Piano • Vocal • Guitar

THE ILLUSTRATED TREASURY OF Disney SONGS

The following songs are the property of:

Bourne Co.
Music Publishers
5 West 37th Street
New York, NY 10018

Baby Mine
Give A Little Whistle
Heigh-Ho
Hi-Diddle-Dee-Dee (An Actor's Life For Me)
I'm Wishing
I've Got No Strings
Some Day My Prince Will Come
When I See An Elephant Fly
When You Wish Upon A Star
Whistle While You Work
Who's Afraid Of The Big Bad Wolf?

ISBN 978-1-5400-1530-3

DISTRIBUTED BY

HAL•LEONARD®

Visit Hal Leonard Online at
www.halleonard.com

Contact Us:
Hal Leonard
7777 West Bluemound Road
Milwaukee, WI 53213
Email: info@halleonard.com

In Europe contact:
Hal Leonard Europe Limited
42 Wigmore Street
Marylebone, London, W1U 2RN
Email: info@halleonardeurope.com

In Australia contact:
Hal Leonard Australia Pty. Ltd.
4 Lentara Court
Cheltenham, Victoria, 3192 Australia
Email: info@halleonard.com.au

CONTENTS

** TARZAN® Owned by Edgar Rice Burroughs, Inc.
and Used by Permission
© Burroughs/Disney

INTRODUCTION

Walt Disney didn't read or write music. In fact, he never even played an instrument, unless you count a brief stab at the violin during grade school in Kansas City.

And yet, his influence upon music was, and continues to be, so profound that the great American composer Jerome Kern was moved to say, "Disney has made use of music as language. In the synchronization of humorous episodes with humorous music, he has unquestionably given us the outstanding contribution of our time."

That's lofty praise, especially coming as it did from a musical legend like Kern. But what makes his words all the more amazing is the fact that he said them in 1936, *before* the release of *Snow White and the Seven Dwarfs*, arguably one of Walt Disney's greatest moments not only in animation, but music history as well.

Still, the question remains: if Walt didn't write any songs or compose any scores, how could he have had such a deep and lasting impact on music? The answer, simply enough, is the same way in which he had such a profound effect upon animation.

Walt was the mover and shaker, the man of vision who gathered around him some of the most talented writers, artists, composers, and musicians, who bought into his dreams and schemes and made them happen, all under his watchful eye.

Walt and Roy Disney with the special "Oscar" awarded to Walt in 1932 for the creation of Mickey Mouse.

Disney's imprimatur is stamped onto every song . . .

He once described his role this way:

> My role? Well, you know I was stumped one day when a little boy asked, "Do you draw Mickey Mouse?" I had to admit I do not draw anymore. "Then you think up the jokes and ideas?" "No," I said, "I don't do that." Finally, he looked at me and said, "Mr. Disney, just what do you do?" "Well," I said, "sometimes I think of myself as a little bee. I go from one area of the Studio to another and gather pollen and sort of stimulate everybody. I guess that's the job I do."

Of course, that doesn't explain Walt Disney's uncanny feel for what worked and what didn't, be it in music, films, or theme parks. Perhaps Eric Sevareid summed it up best in his tribute to Walt on the *CBS Evening News* the day Disney died: "He was an original; not just an American original, but an original, period. He was a happy accident; one of the happiest this century has experienced… People are saying we'll never see his like again."

Maybe it was his Midwestern upbringing and mid-American, mainstream appreciation for music and movies, or maybe he was just "a happy accident," but Walt Disney aimed to create entertainment that he himself would enjoy. Could he help it if hundreds of millions of people around the world happened to agree with him?

So although he didn't write "When You Wish Upon a Star," "Zip-A-Dee-Doo-Dah," or any of the other hundreds of tunes that make up the Disney canon, his imprimatur is stamped onto every song and score. When you hear "Whistle While You Work," you may not know that the words were written by Larry Morey and the music by Frank Churchill, but you certainly know it's a Disney song.

It didn't matter what a composer's background was, whether he was a honky-tonk pianist from Los Angeles, a jingle writer from New York's Tin Pan Alley, or a pop star from England, when someone wrote for Walt Disney, that person wrote in a style that was, consciously or not, immediately recognizable as Walt Disney's.

"No matter what I or anyone else in the music department wrote, people always recognized it as being the 'Disney sound,'" says Buddy Baker, Disney Legend and longtime staff composer. "But if I was asked to define the Disney sound or how we got it, I would have to answer that I didn't know. It's not something I thought about while I was writing the music. I think a clue to the Disney sound, though, comes from the man himself," he adds. "Walt Disney had a wonderful concept of what the music should be, which is a great clue for the composer. For instance, if he wanted a big, symphonic score, he'd tell you that and he'd even tell you what he'd want it to sound like."

Disney songs represent a style and sprightliness that makes them eminently hummable and totally unforgettable. They were very much a reflection of their patron, who concentrated on melody and didn't like anything that was too loud or high-pitched.

Music lightens a story session in the mid 1930s as Walt Disney visits (from left) Webb Smith, Ted Sears, and Pinto Colvig.

Even the "Disney" songs and scores being written today, decades after Walt Disney's death, reflect the spirit and influence of this man who had a special ability to recognize what kind of music best fit a scene or situation and, more importantly (and more to the point), what was good.

It was Walt's direction and influence that led his composers and musicians to pioneer musical concepts and technologies that influenced both the film and music industries for decades—and continue to do so to this day.

But the music did not start out as Disney's own. In the first several Mickey Mouse cartoons, produced in 1928 and 1929, the music was either borrowed or adapted. An example was Mickey's very first cartoon, *Steamboat Willie*, released in November, 1928, and featuring the songs "Steamboat Bill" and "Turkey in the Straw."

(Top) Walt Disney's classic portrait with Mickey Mouse, taken at Disney's Woking Way home in Los Angeles, c.1931.

(Right) In 1938, Disney purchased undeveloped property in Burbank, which soon became the new permanent home to The Walt Disney Studios.

Walt created entertainment that he himself would enjoy.

Still, even if the music wasn't written by members of Walt's staff, it was arranged in such a way that it sounded as if it just might have been. For instance, "Steamboat Bill," written in 1910, was whistled by the mouse himself during the opening moments of the cartoon.

THE EARLY YEARS

The sound that played the key role in Disney cartoons was music.

"Turkey in the Straw," which dates as far back as 1834 and is arguably a sing-song classic in the tradition of "Camptown Races" and "My Darling Clementine," was not arranged for normal instruments, such as guitars, flutes, or pianos, but was instead configured to accommodate the variety of "instruments" Mickey plays during the cartoon, including a washboard, pots and pans, a cat, a duck, several suckling pigs, and a cow's teeth. ("Turkey in the Straw," by the way, was selected for *Steamboat Willie* because it was one of the only tunes a young assistant animator named Wilfred Jackson, the sole musician at the small Disney studio, could play on the harmonica.)

It could be said that the Disney musical legacy began with Walt himself. In 1929, he teamed with his then-musical director Carl Stalling to write a song that would become an anthem of sorts for his already famous star, Mickey Mouse.

That song, "Minnie's Yoo Hoo," was first heard in the 1929 short "Mickey's Follies." It is the only song for which Walt Disney ever took a writing credit.

Mickey Mouse and the musical improvisation that made him famous in his debut film, Steamboat Willie.

It was Stalling who persuaded Walt to begin the Silly Symphony cartoon series, which grew out of disagreements the two had over the use of music in the Mickey Mouse shorts. Walt wanted Stalling to fit the music to the action, while Stalling felt the action should fit the music.

The Silly Symphonies were a compromise. In the Mickey cartoons, the music would continue to play second fiddle to the characters and the action, but in the Silly Symphonies the music would rule.

Stalling stayed with the Studio less than two years, jumping from Silly Symphonies at Disney to Looney Tunes and Merrie Melodies at Warner Brothers, where he created his own musical legacy, composing scores for the likes of Bugs Bunny, Daffy Duck, and Porky Pig.

But that doesn't mean Walt didn't play an active role in the creation of the music heard in all succeeding Disney studio cartoon shorts and animated features. He simply entrusted it to more accomplished composers and arrangers, the first of which was Stalling, an old friend from Kansas City.

Despite Stalling's departure, the Silly Symphonies continued. In fact, they became so popular that Walt Disney began beefing up his music staff in the early '30s to handle the increased need for music for them.

In "Silly Symphonies" the music would rule.

The surprise hit song from Three Little Pigs *spawned a range of merchandise, including (left to right) sheet music, a board game, and records. These rare 1933 items are treasured by collectors today.*

One of the composers he hired was Frank Churchill, a young musician who had studied at UCLA and gained experience playing honky-tonk piano in Mexico and performing on a Los Angeles radio station (as well as serving as a session player in recording sessions for Disney cartoons). This heretofore unsung musician would play an important role in Disney music over the next decade. And he started off with a bang, writing Disney's first big hit, a song that came out of perhaps the most famous of the Silly Symphonies, *Three Little Pigs*.

Released in 1933 during the depths of the Depression, *Three Little Pigs* and its famous song, "Who's Afraid of the Big Bad Wolf?" provided hope and humor to a country that was badly in need of both.

As with many Disney films, *Three Little Pigs* comes from a children's story. But to Churchill, it also represented real life. While growing up on his family's ranch in San Luis Obispo, California, he was given three little piglets to raise by his mother. All went well until a real "Big Bad Wolf" killed one of them.

As legend has it, when Churchill was asked to write a song for the cartoon, he recalled his horrifying childhood experience and penned "Who's Afraid of the Big Bad Wolf?" in about five minutes, patterning the song loosely on "Happy Birthday." When it was released as a single and in sheet music, it featured additional lyrics by Ann Ronell.

"Who's Afraid of the Big Bad Wolf?" provided hope and humor to a country that was badly in need of both.

With "Who's Afraid of the Big Bad Wolf?" Walt Disney and his staff had created their first sing-a-long classic. It certainly would not be their last.

In 1929, the Disney studio's creative team included (standing from left) Johnny Cannon, Walt Disney, Burt Gillett, Ub Iwerks, Wilfred Jackson, Les Clark; (seated from left) Carl Stalling, Jack King, and Ben Sharpsteen.

A COMING OF AGE

$\mathcal{T}$he next step for Walt Disney and his staff was the creation of the first full-length animated feature. But Walt wasn't content to "just" create and produce a feature-length cartoon. He envisioned something more.

From its beginnings, *Snow White and the Seven Dwarfs* was planned around music. However, early attempts at songs did not satisfy Walt. He complained that they were too much in the vein of so many Hollywood musicals that introduced songs without regard to the story. "We should set a new pattern, a new way to use music," he told his staff. "Weave it into the story so somebody doesn't just burst into song."

That last line, as simply stated as it is, has been the guiding principle in Disney animated features from *Snow White* and *Pinocchio* all the way through the more recent efforts, including *The Lion King*, *Tangled*, and *Frozen*.

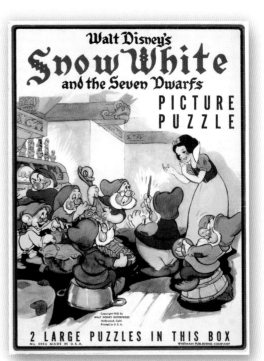

What Walt wanted with *Snow White and the Seven Dwarfs* was something closer to Broadway musical than Hollywood motion picture.

Frank Churchill and Larry Morey were assigned the task of writing the songs for *Snow White*. By the time all was said and sung, the pair had written 25 songs, only eight of which ended up in the film. But what an eight they were, each one a classic in its own right.

The first original motion picture soundtrack record album was Snow White and the Seven Dwarfs, *released by Victor Records in 1937.*

We should set a new pattern, a new way to use music.

Walt Disney didn't write any songs for *Snow White*, but he played an active role in defining the content of each song and how it would fit into the film, as these notes from a story conference on "Whistle While You Work" demonstrate:

> Change words of a song so they fit in more with Snow White's handing the animals brushes, etc. Snow White: "If you just hum a merry tune"…and they start humming. Then Snow White would start to tell them to "whistle while you work." She would start giving the animals things to do. By that time, she has sung, of course… Birds would come marching in. Try to arrange to stay with the birds for a section of whistling. Orchestra would play with a whistling effect…get it in the woodwinds…like playing something instrumentally to sound like whistling…

> Get a way to finish the song that isn't just an end. Work in a shot trucking [moving] out of the house. Truck back and show animals shaking rugs out of the windows…little characters outside beating things out in the yard…

> Truck out and the melody of "Whistle While You Work" gets quieter and quieter. Leave them all working. The last thing you see as you truck away is little birds hanging out clothes. Fade out on that and music would fade out. At the end, all you would hear is the flute—before fading into the "Dig Dig" song [which precedes the song "Heigh-Ho"] and the hammering rhythm.

Snow White and the Seven Dwarfs ushered in not only the Golden Age of Disney Animation in the late 1930s and early 1940s, but the Golden Age of Disney Music as well. While Disney's animators were creating some of the most beautiful screen images ever seen, the studio's composers were producing some of the most memorable songs ever heard, including "When You Wish Upon a Star" from *Pinocchio* (1940), "Baby Mine" from *Dumbo* (1941), and "Little April Shower" from *Bambi* (1942).

World War II brought an abrupt end to the Golden Age. At The Walt Disney Studios, the emphasis changed from creating animated features to producing cartoon shorts and instructional films to aid the war effort. Even after the war was over, Walt Disney didn't immediately return to animated features. Instead, he concentrated on "package" pictures (movies that featured a series of animated shorts rolled into one motion picture) and films featuring both live-action and animation.

But Disney's staff of composers continued to play a significant role in these efforts, writing such memorable tunes as the Latin-influenced "Saludos Amigos" and "You Belong to My Heart" from the two South American travelog-style films *Saludos Amigos* (1943) and *The Three Caballeros* (1945), "The Lord Is Good to Me" from *Melody Time* (1948), and one of the most popular Disney songs ever written, "Zip-A-Dee-Doo-Dah," the irresistibly upbeat tune from *Song of the South* (1946).

Composer Frank Churchill (left) and sequence director/lyricist Larry Morey in the mid 1930s creating songs for Snow White and the Seven Dwarfs.

SONGS FROM TIN PAN ALLEY

*I*n 1950, Walt Disney returned to animated features with the release of *Cinderella*, but instead of relying on his music staff for the film's song score, he turned to writers from New York's Tin Pan Alley, something he would continue to do for his animated features throughout the 1950s.

Originally 28th Street in Manhattan, Tin Pan Alley was home to many of the largest song publishers in the United States. Each publisher employed an army of songwriters who worked out of small offices furnished with nothing more than pianos and music stands. During the summer, the writers would open their windows in a futile effort to get some relief from the stifling New York heat (the buildings weren't air conditioned). The noise of the pianos echoing through the street gave one the impression of people banging on tin pans, hence the name "Tin Pan Alley."

Walt didn't consciously set out to use Tin Pan Alley writers for *Cinderella*. While in New York on business prior to the start of production, he kept hearing on the radio a catchy novelty song, "Chi-Baba Chi-Baba," written by the team of Mack David, Jerry Livingston, and Al Hoffman. He was so taken with the song that he ended up hiring the trio to write the songs for *Cinderella*. Perhaps it's no surprise, then, that one of the songs, "Bibbidi-Bobbidi-Boo (The Magic Song)," is in the same vein as "Chi-Baba."

Walt again turned to Tin Pan Alley for *Alice in Wonderland* (1951), primarily because he felt the film would need an abundance of novelty songs, something the Tin Pan Alley gang was quite adept at producing. In all, 14 songs were written for *Alice*, including "I'm Late," one of nine tunes written for the film by Bob Hilliard and Sammy Fain, and "The Unbirthday Song" contributed by the *Cinderella* trio of David, Hoffman, and Livingston.

The renaissance in Disney animation continued through the 1950s and early 1960s with the release of such animated features as *Peter Pan* (1953), *Lady and the Tramp* (1955), *Sleeping Beauty* (1959), and *101 Dalmatians* (1961). The bulk of the songs continued to be written by Tin Pan Alley tunesmiths, such as Sammy Cahn, Sammy Fain, and Jack Lawrence. The notable exception was *Lady and the Tramp*, which featured songs by Peggy Lee and Sonny Burke.

The increasing reliance on outside writers for songs for the animated features presented no danger to the jobs of Disney's crack staff of composers and arrangers. At least they didn't seem worried by it, perhaps because they were so busy.

Walt demanded quality, whether it was music for a multi-million dollar animated feature or a television show.

"[The 1950s were] a hectic time at the studio," recalls Buddy Baker, who joined the Disney music staff following a career in big bands and radio. "We had the weekly series [*Disneyland*, which later became *The Wonderful World of Disney*, among other titles] to write music for, plus the daily show [*Mickey Mouse Club*]. This was in addition to the feature films the studio was producing. And Walt demanded quality, whether it was music for a multi-million dollar animated feature or a television show."

Walt's staff of composers was so busy writing the music they often turned to anyone who was ready, willing, and able to write the lyrics, be they animators, scriptwriters, story editors, or, in the case of "Old Yeller," studio nurses (the lyrics for that song are credited to Gil George, who was in fact Disney studio nurse Hazel George).

Disney staffers at the time included music director Oliver Wallace ("Old Yeller" and "Pretty Irish Girl"), Jimmie Dodd ("The Mickey Mouse March"), and George Bruns ("Zorro" and "The Ballad of Davy Crockett").

Bruns's experience writing "The Ballad of Davy Crockett" for the *Davy Crockett* series of TV shows was typical of the way songs were written for Walt Disney in the harried '50s, though the results were far from typical.

"Walt needed what I call a little 'throwaway' tune that would bridge the time gaps in the story of Davy Crockett," recalled Bruns. "He needed a song that would carry the story from one sequence to another. I threw together the melody line and chorus, 'Davy, Davy Crockett, King of the Wild Frontier,' in about 30 minutes."

Composer George Bruns created a diverse range of music for Disney, from the award-winning score for Sleeping Beauty *to the hit song "The Ballad of Davy Crockett."*

Tom Blackburn, the scriptwriter for the *Davy Crockett* series, had never before written a song, but that didn't stop him from adding the lyrics, 120 lines of them (the completed version has 20 stanzas of six lines each).

Even before the television series went on the air, "The Ballad of Davy Crockett" took the country by storm. Bruns and Blackburn's little "throwaway" tune became a national sensation, much as racoon-skin caps would when the show premiered.

"It certainly took everybody at the studio by surprise," said Bruns. "The irony of it was that most people thought it was an authentic folk song that we had uncovered and updated. Usually when you have a hit song, there are always lawsuits claiming prior authorship. In the case of 'Davy Crockett,' not a single suit was filed."

"The Ballad of Davy Crockett" became the fastest-selling record of 1955.

THE SHERMANS MARCH THROUGH DISNEY

*I*f the 1950s were characterized by Walt Disney's reliance on Tin Pan Alley songwriters, the trend in the 1960s could be summed up in two words: Sherman Brothers.

Hired by Walt Disney in 1961 as staff songwriters, Richard M. and Robert B. Sherman proved versatile and prolific during their almost decade-long association with Disney, writing more than 200 songs, many of which have become timeless classics.

Perhaps the greatest achievement of the Sherman Brothers' Disney career came in 1964 with the release of *Mary Poppins*, for which they wrote 14 songs and earned two Academy Awards®, one for Best Song ("Chim Chim Cher-ee") and the other for Best Song Score.

"Writing songs for *Mary Poppins* was a songwriter's dream. Each song we did had a purpose, a reason for being," says Robert Sherman, echoing the long-held philosophy of Walt Disney about music in motion pictures.

Typical of their experiences composing tunes for *Mary Poppins* was the inspiration behind one of the most popular and memorable tunes in the film, "Supercalifragilisticexpialidocious."

"When we were little boys in summer camp in the Catskill Mountains in the mid 1930s," explains Richard Sherman, "we heard this word. Not the exact word, but a word very similar to 'supercal.' It was a word that was longer than

Supercalifragilisticexpialidocious

The pair penned songs for animated features (*The Sword and the Stone* [1963], *The Jungle Book* [1967], *The Aristocats* [1970]) and featurettes (*Winnie the Pooh and the Honey Tree* [1966]), live-action musicals (*Summer Magic* [1963], *The Happiest Millionaire* [1967]), live-action non-musicals (*The Parent Trap* [1961], *In Search of the Castaways* [1962], *The Monkey's Uncle* [1965], *That Darn Cat* [1965]), musicals combining live-action and animation (*Bedknobs and Broomsticks* [1971]), theme parks (*Walt Disney's Enchanted Tiki Room* [1963]), and even the 1964-65 New York World's Fair (*Carousel of Progress*, *It's a Small World*).

'antidisestablishmentarianism,' and it gave us kids a word that no adult had. It was our own special word, and we wanted the Banks children to have that same feeling."

Songwriters Richard Sherman (left) and Robert Sherman (right) review the music for Mary Poppins *with the film's co-producer and writer, Bill Walsh (center).*

Mary Poppins also proved to be the crowning achievement of Walt Disney's long and storied motion picture career. Combining live-action, animation, and the Sherman Brothers song score, it was the culmination of everything he'd been working toward in his more than 40 years in the film business.

When Walt Disney passed away on December 15, 1966, there was concern that his studio would not be able to survive without him. But Walt had confidence it would. "I think by this time my staff…[is] convinced that Walt is right, that quality will win out," he once said. "And so I think they're going to stay with that policy because it's proved that it's a good business policy… I think they're convinced and I think they'll hang on, as you say, after Disney."

Throughout the 1970s and 1980s The Walt Disney Studios continued producing animated and live-action features, but all of them, with the exceptions of *Robin Hood* (1973) and *Pete's Dragon* (1977), were non-musicals. That didn't mean there weren't any songs in Disney movies. Such animated features as *The Rescuers* (1977) did feature songs, but these songs were usually performed during the opening or closing credits and were not essential to the story.

A MUSICAL RENAISSANCE

All that changed in 1988 with the release of *Oliver & Company*, Disney's first full-scale animated musical in more than a decade.

The film featured five tunes written by a Who's Who of pop songwriters, including Barry Manilow, Dan Hartman, and Dean Pitchford. But the key was that all of the songs adhered to an old Disney maxim: music should play an integral and prominent part in the story without overshadowing or disrupting it.

"Music should come out of the dialogue," said the film's director, George Scribner, reemphasizing a point Walt Disney had made many times

Animation is the last great place to do Broadway musicals.

years before. "The best music advances the story or defines a character. The challenge was to figure out areas in our film where music could better express a concept or idea."

Perhaps no one knew this better than a New York-based lyricist named Howard Ashman, who co-wrote "Once Upon a Time in New York City" for *Oliver & Company*.

With his longtime writing partner Alan Menken, Ashman redefined and revitalized the animated musical, bringing to it a style, wit, and sophistication that hadn't been seen or heard since the early 1940s.

"Animation is the last great place to do Broadway musicals," said Ashman, explaining the inspiration for *The Little Mermaid* (1989), *Beauty and the Beast* (1991), and *Aladdin* (1992). "It's a place you can use a whole other set of skills and a way of working which is more the way plays and musicals are made. With most films, the story seems to come first and the songs are an afterthought.

"Coming from a musical theater background," he continued, "Alan and I are used to writing songs for characters in situations. For *The Little Mermaid* we wanted songs that would really move the story forward and keep things driving ahead."

The seven songs Ashman and Menken wrote for the film did that and more. The result was the beginning of a New Golden Age of Animation that continues to this day.

Ashman and Menken followed the success of *The Little Mermaid* (for which they won an Academy Award for "Under the Sea") with *Beauty and the Beast*.

A review of the film in *Newsweek* magazine says it all: "The most delicious musical score of 1991 is Alan Menken and Howard Ashman's *Beauty and the Beast*. If the growing armada of titanically troubled Broadway musicals had half its charm and affectionate cleverness, the ships wouldn't be foundering."

The duo wrote six songs for the film, including an unprecedented three songs that were nominated for Academy Awards®: "Be Our Guest," "Belle," and the eventual Oscar®-winner "Beauty and the Beast."

Before his death in March of 1991, Ashman had written lyrics for three songs in the next big Disney animated feature, *Aladdin*, including "Friend Like Me." Once again, the composer was Alan Menken. For the rest of the score, Menken collaborated with lyricist Tim Rice, a theatre veteran who, earlier in his career, wrote *Evita* and *Jesus Christ Superstar* with Andrew Lloyd Webber. Menken, Rice, and the film were honored with an Academy Award® for Best Song for "A Whole New World."

Disney's live-action musical tradition continued with the 1992 release of *Newsies*, a full-scale production about the organization of newsboys in New York early in the 20th century. The score, by Alan Menken and Jack Feldman, includes the boys' inspirational anthem, "Seize the Day."

As the 1990s continued, Disney reaffirmed its place as the world's best producer of beautiful and successful animated films. The next animated musical, released in 1994, was the universally beloved *The Lion King*, the allegorical story of the love between a lion cub and his father. Tim Rice was signed first to write the lyrics. "The studio asked me if I had any suggestions as to who could write the music. They said, 'Choose anybody in the world and choose the best.' I said, 'Well, Elton John would be fantastic.'" The producers were at first hesitant to approach the legendary rock star, but as it turned out, he was

The songwriting team of Howard Ashman (left) and Alan Menken received Academy Awards® for their work on The Little Mermaid *and* Beauty and the Beast.

anxious to come on board. "I actually jumped at the chance," John confessed, "because I knew that Disney was a class act and I liked the story line and the people immediately."

Has there ever been a musical number on film, live or animated, that surpasses the emotional beauty of the opening number, "Circle of Life"? Rice, who first wrote the words for the song, was amazed at the speed with which Elton John composed. "I gave him the lyrics at the beginning of the session at about two in the afternoon. By half-past three, he'd finished writing and recording a stunning demo." Disney added another Academy Award® to its collection when "Can You Feel the Love Tonight?" was cited as Best Song.

Pocahontas was the first Disney animated feature inspired by factual history. It brought another major theatre talent into The Walt Disney Studios in Stephen Schwartz, who wrote the lyrics for the score, with music once again by Alan Menken. Schwartz knew success at a young age on Broadway as the composer and lyricist of *Godspell* and *Pippin*. The combined talents of Menken and Schwartz produced yet another Academy Award® for Best Song for "Colors of the Wind," a chart-topping hit for singer Vanessa Williams.

Toy Story, the first full-length feature film animated entirely on computers, takes place among the magical lives of a six-year-old's collection of toys. A special film like this needed a unique kind of song, and Pixar found that in singer-songwriter Randy Newman. "You've Got a Friend in Me" is the chummy song that expresses the easy goodwill of the enchanting story of Woody, Buzz, and Andy.

Alan Menken's sixth score for Disney was another collaboration with Stephen Schwartz—the adaptation of the classic 19th century Victor Hugo novel *The Hunchback of Notre Dame*. This was an incredibly ambitious undertaking in every regard. Just the task of adapting a screenplay from the sprawling novel is difficult enough, but creating a satisfying animated musical from this complicated story was a monumental task. The resulting critically acclaimed film is evidence of just how splendidly all those involved succeeded. The score contains an extensive, expressive collection of songs borrowing influences from gypsy music, French music, and traditional liturgical music. The richly emotional songs include "God Help the Outcasts," which, beyond the film score was recorded by Bette Midler, and "Someday," which became a hit for the vocal group All-4-One.

For *Hercules*, Disney turned to a new source for a story: ancient Greek mythology. But this was no dull classroom textbook topic as realized by The Walt Disney Studios. The film is a marvelously entertaining tale of the triumph of a true hero, enlivened by new songs, once again by Alan Menken, with lyrics by David Zippel, a Tony® Award winner for his work on the Broadway musical *City of Angels*. Rock singer Michael Bolton had a hit single with the expansive, soaring "Go the Distance," certainly an anthem befitting the mighty son of Zeus.

In 1989, Disney developed an animation studio in Orlando, Walt Disney Feature Animation Florida. *Mulan* was the first feature film largely created there using then-amazing state-of-the-art computer-assisted animation. This 2,000-year-old tale is of a courageous young Chinese woman who enters the army disguised as a man so that her ailing father can be spared military service. Technology allowed panoramic camera effects never before possible in animation, with especially amazing crowd scenes and the attack of the Huns. The songs, by Matthew Wilder and David Zippel, include "Reflection" and "Honor to Us All."

One of the most exciting developments at Disney has been the expansion of the company's business to include Broadway musicals. *Beauty and the Beast* was adapted for the stage in vivid fashion, with additional songs by Alan Menken and Tim Rice. The show opened on Broadway on April 18, 1994, and became the tenth longest-running show in Broadway history. A touring company of the musical has been a smash success on the road.

Disney's claim to a piece of Broadway became even more tangible with the renovation of the New Amsterdam Theatre. Built in 1903 and restored to its original splendor, it is now a cornerstone in the major redevelopment of 42nd Street in New York. The New Amsterdam became home to *The Lion King*, one of the most innovative musicals ever to open on The Great White Way. The stage adaptation from the animated film opened on Broadway on November 13, 1997, and contains additional songs by Disney Legends Sir Elton John and Sir Tim Rice, as well as songs by Hans Zimmer, Lebo M, Mark Mancina, Disney Legend Julie Taymor, and Jay Rifkin. The stunning production was also directed and co-designed by cutting-edge talent Julie Taymor. The

© Disney, Original Dutch Cast, photo by Deen van Meer

musical won the 1998 Tony® Award for Best Musical, and has become the third longest-running show ever on Broadway.

On the heels of its Broadway success with *The Lion King*, Disney triumphed once again with another Elton John/Tim Rice collaboration, 1999's *Aida*. Inspired by the Verdi opera of the same name, *Aida* is the story of Egyptian prince and war-hero Radames, who, although betrothed to Princess Amneris, enters into a forbidden romance with the war-captured Aida, herself also, but secretly, of royal bloodlines. The play captured four Tony® Awards in 2000, including Best Original Musical Score, and a Grammy® that same year for Best Musical Show Album. A single of one of the show's most beloved songs, "Written in the Stars," as recorded by Sir Elton John and LeAnn Rimes, reached No. 2 on Billboard's Adult Contemporary Charts and No. 4 in Canada.

That same year, Disney released two hugely successful animated features: *Tarzan*™, an adaptation of the Edgar Rice Burroughs classic, and *Toy Story 2*, a follow-up to the 1995 landmark computer-animated blockbuster. Scored by pop-rocker and longtime Genesis band member and Disney Legend Phil Collins, the *Tarzan*™ soundtrack included the world beat infused "Two Worlds," and the No. 1 Adult Contemporary hit "You'll Be in My Heart," which beat out Randy Newman's *Toy Story 2* nominated song "When She Loved Me" to win the 1999 Academy Award® for Best Original Song from a Motion Picture.

A NEW GENERATION

With the new century came new Disney escapades—including 2001's *Monsters, Inc.*, the fourth feature film by computer-animation giant Pixar Animation Studios, following *Toy Story, Toy Story 2*, and *A Bug's Life*. The film is about two monsters who, as employees of a scream-inducing factory called Monsters, Inc., frighten children and "collect" their screams which then provide power to the monsters' city. *Monsters Inc.* garnered an Oscar® for Best Original Song for composer/lyricist Randy Newman's "If I Didn't Have You."

Swashbuckling made an enormous comeback with Disney's live-action *Pirates of the Caribbean* films. Born as a Disneyland attraction in 1967, the Pirates phenomenon hit the big screen in 2003 with *Pirates of the Caribbean: The Curse of the Black Pearl*. Disney's first PG-13 film, it featured sweeping, original music by Klaus Badelt. Four more *Pirates* films followed: *Dead Man's Chest* in 2006, *At World's End* in 2007, *On Stranger Tides* in 2011, and *Dead Men Tell No Tales* in 2017.

The Incredibles features animation as only Pixar can do it. The 2004 feature film finds a pair of retired superheroes raising a family in quiet, suburban anonymity, but yearning for adventure. When evil rears its ugly head, the family, foibles and all, is spurred to heroic action to save the day. Michael Giacchino's jazzy, splashy "The Incredits," won a Grammy® for Best Instrumental Arrangement.

Hand-drawn Disney animation returned to the big screen in 2007 with *Enchanted*. Mixing artful traditional animation techniques, computer-generated fantasy, the realism of live-action and the music and lyrics of Alan Menken and Stephen Schwartz, the film finds a fairy-tale princess dropped into the middle of New York City's Times Square. Her handsome prince follows to rescue her, as does a good deal of magic and charm.

UP is a 2009 heart-warming tale of a widower longing to make the trip to an exotic land that he and his late wife never got around to completing. Michael Giacchino's "Married Life," played behind a tear-jerking montage of the couple's happy life together, won the Grammy® for Best Instrumental Composition.

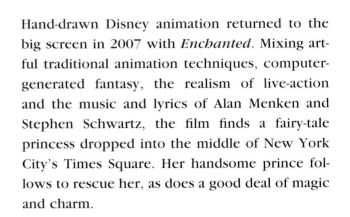

2009 saw the resurgence of a classic Disney story-telling technique: using traditional fairy tales. *The Princess and the Frog* is loosely based on the classic tale, "The Frog Prince," and was soon joined by 2010's *Tangled* (based on "Rapunzel"). *Frozen*, the 2013 film inspired by Hans Christian Andersen's "The Snow Queen", won Academy Awards® for Best Animated Feature and for Best Original Song, for "Let It Go."

I cannot think of the pictorial story without thinking about the complementary music that will fulfill it...

Lava is a Pixar short, which played in theaters before the 2015 film *Inside Out*. *Lava* tells the story of a lonely volcano searching for his love. After years of singing about his search, he eventually vents his lava and sinks into the ocean, only to discover that an undersea volcano heard his singing all along and has fallen in love with him. They both rise above the sea and enjoy their new-found love together.

Moana is a 2016 film from Walt Disney Animation Studios telling the story of a chief's daughter from Oceania on a quest to save her people. Along the way, she finds Maui, a less-than-humble demigod, and eventually discovers her true identity.

Beauty and the Beast returned to the big screen in 2017, this time as a live-action film. It includes many Alan Menken and Howard Ashman songs from the 1991 movie, with several additional songs by Menken and lyrics by Tim Rice, including the stirring ballad "Evermore."

In Disney/Pixar's *Coco* (2017), an aspiring young musician named Miguel embarks on an extraordinary journey to the magical land of his ancestors. There, a charming trickster becomes an unexpected friend who helps Miguel uncover the mysteries behind his family's stories and traditions. "Remember Me" is a recurring song throughout the movie, connecting generations together. It won the Academy Award® for Best Original Song, the second for Kristen Anderson-Lopez and Robert Lopez (after "Let It Go" from *Frozen*).

Walt Disney, 1944

Perhaps it was Walt Disney himself who best summed up the reasons for the important role and the incredible success music has enjoyed in Disney animated features, live-action motion pictures, Boadway musicals, and theme parks:

"Music has always had a prominent part in all our products from the early cartoon days. So much so, in fact, that I cannot think of the pictorial story without thinking about the complementary music that will fulfill it… I have had no formal musical training. But by long experience and by strong personal leaning, I've selected musical themes, original or adapted, that were guided to wide audience acceptance.

"But credit for the memorable songs and scores must, of course, go to the brilliant composers and musicians who have been associated with me through the years."

Who's Afraid of the Big Bad Wolf?

From *THREE LITTLE PIGS*

Words and Music by FRANK CHURCHILL
Additional Lyric by ANN RONELL

Lyrics:
Who's a-fraid of the big bad wolf, big bad wolf, big bad wolf? Who's a-fraid of the big bad wolf? Tra-la-la-la-la. la. Long a-go there were three pigs, lit-tle hand-some pig-gy-wigs, for the big bad, ver-y big

ver - y bad _ wolf, they _ did - n't give three figs. Num - ber one was ver - y gay, and he

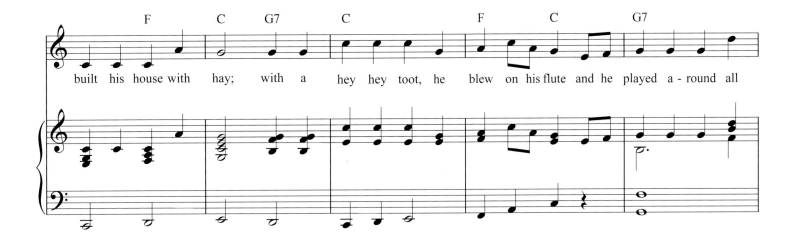

built his house with hay; with a hey hey toot, he blew on his flute and he played a - round all

day. Who's a - fraid of the big bad wolf, big bad wolf,

big bad wolf? Who's a - fraid of the big bad wolf? Tra - la - la - la - la.

Minnie's Yoo Hoo

From *MICKEY'S FOLLIES*

Words by WALT DISNEY and CARL STALLING
Music by CARL STALLING

I'm the guy they call lit - tle Mick - ey Mouse, got a
blue bird call down in the cher - ry tree, got and the

sweet - ie down in the chick - en house, neith - er fat nor skin - ny, she's the
bu - sy buzz of the bum - ble bee, eve - ning bells a - ring - in', whip - poor-

hors - e's whin - ny, she's my lit - tle Min - nie Mouse. When it's
wills a - sing - in', well, they don't mean much to me. For my

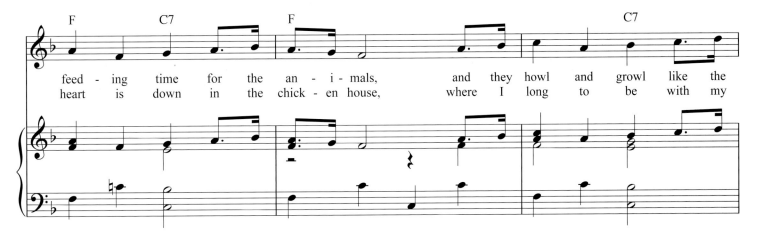

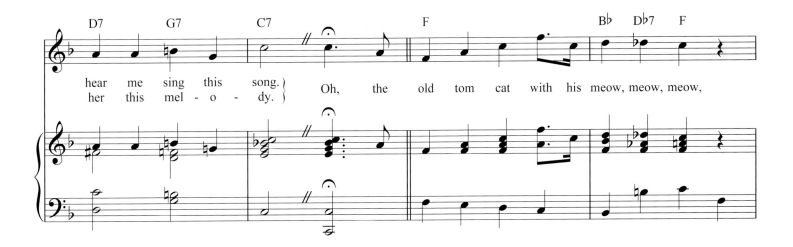

mule's hee - haw, gosh what a rack - et like an old buzz saw. I have

lis - tened to the Koo - koo kook his koo - koo, and I've heard the roost - er cock his doo - dle

doo doo. With the cows and the chick - ens, all sound like the dick - ens, when I

hear my lit - tle Min - nie's yoo hoo. Oh, the yoo hoo.

I'm Wishing

From *SNOW WHITE AND THE SEVEN DWARFS*

Words by LARRY MOREY
Music by FRANK CHURCHILL

It's so sad and lone-ly, wish-ing well, _____ long-ing for some-one you nev-er see. _____ Make him love me on-ly, wish-ing well, _____ won't you grant this fa-vor to

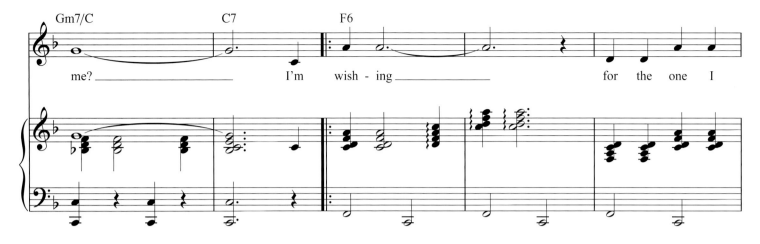

me? _____ I'm wish - ing _____ for the one I

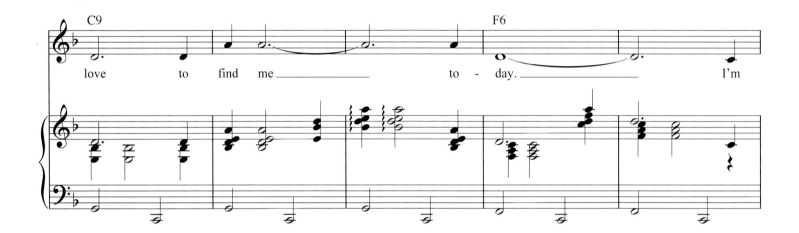

love to find me _____ to - day. _____ I'm

hop - ing, _____ and I'm dream - ing of the nice things _____

___ he'll say. _____ Tell me, wish - ing well, _____

will my wish come true? _____ With your mag - ic spell, _____

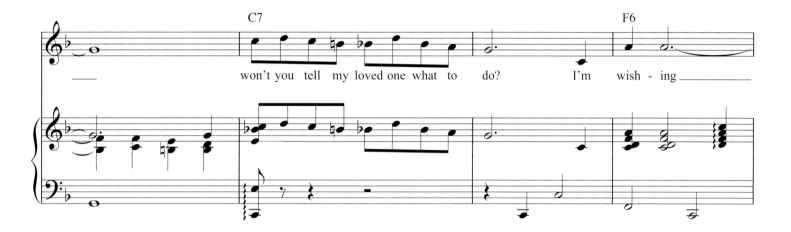

won't you tell my loved one what to do? I'm wish - ing _____

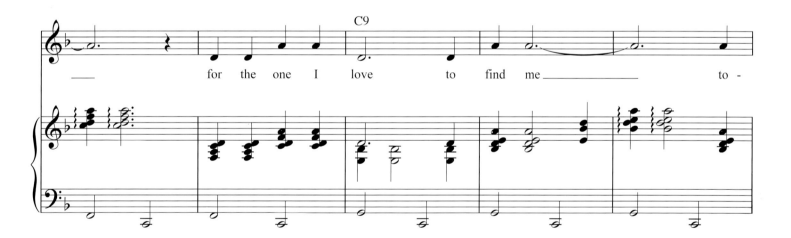

for the one I love to find me _____ to -

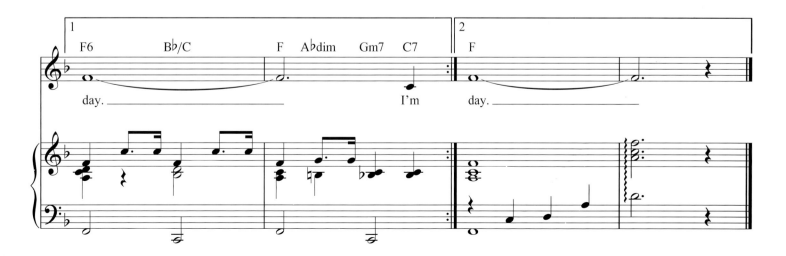

day. _____ I'm day. _____

Heigh-Ho

From *SNOW WHITE AND THE SEVEN DWARFS*

Words by LARRY MOREY
Music by FRANK CHURCHILL

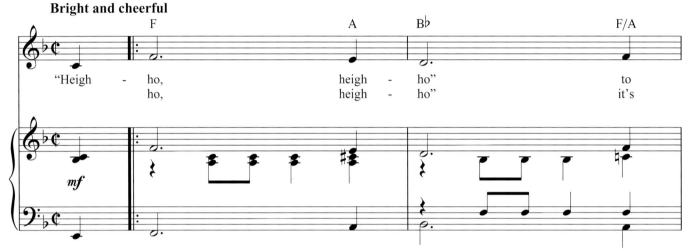

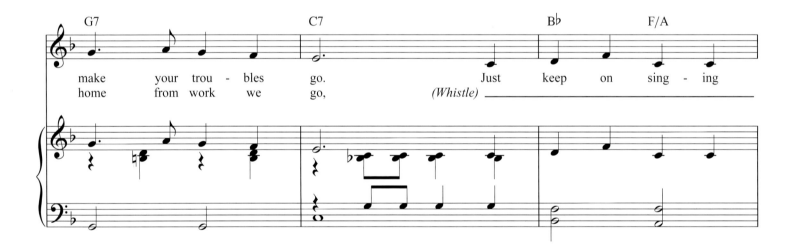

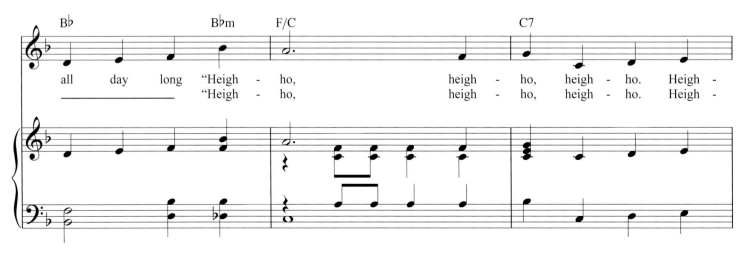

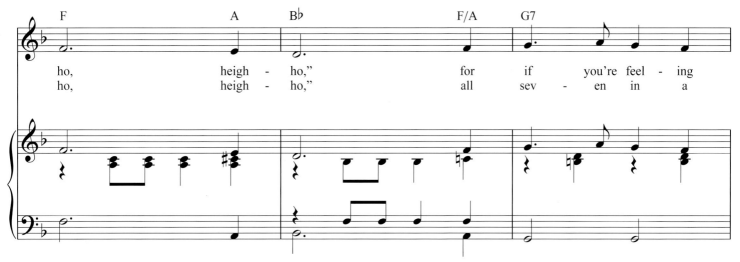

ho, heigh - ho," for if you're feel - ing
ho, heigh - ho," all sev - en in a

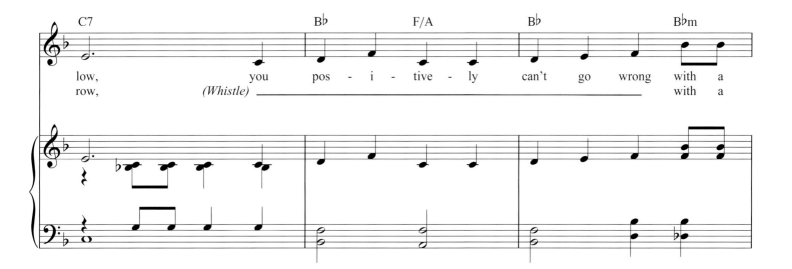

low, you pos - i - tive - ly can't go wrong with a
row, *(Whistle)* _____ with a

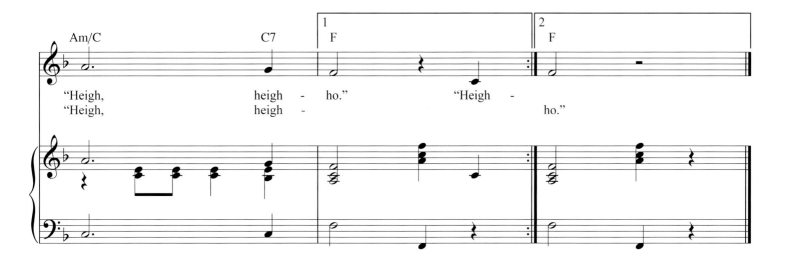

"Heigh, heigh - ho." "Heigh -
"Heigh, heigh - ho."

Some Day My Prince Will Come

From *SNOW WHITE AND THE SEVEN DWARFS*

Words by LARRY MOREY
Music by FRANK CHURCHILL

Rather fast

Some day my prince will come, some
Some day I'll find my love, some -

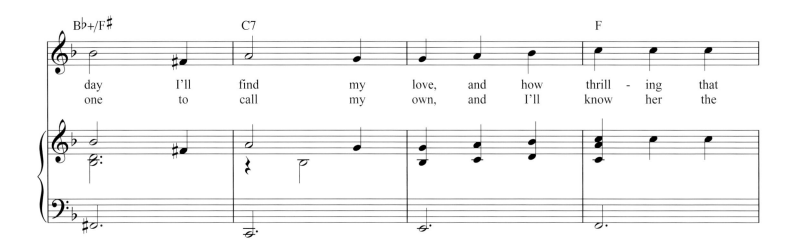

day I'll find my love, and how thrill - ing that
one to call my own, and how I'll know her the

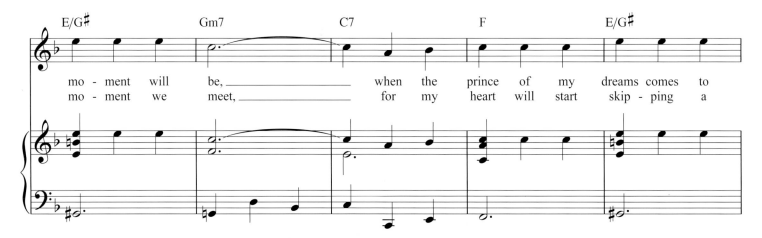

mo - ment will be, _____ when the prince of my dreams comes to
mo - ment we meet, _____ for my heart will start skip - ping a

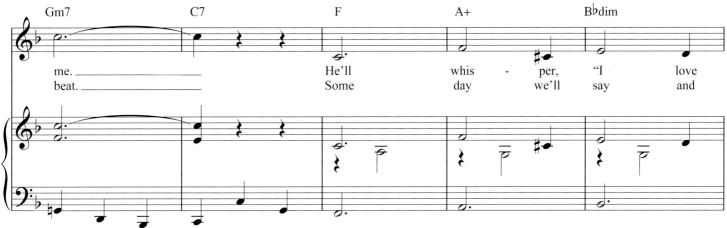

me. _____ He'll whis - per, "I love
beat. _____ Some day we'll say and

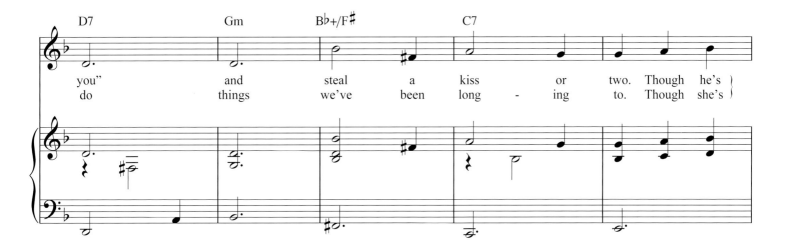

you" and steal a kiss or two. Though he's
do and things we've been long - ing to. Though she's

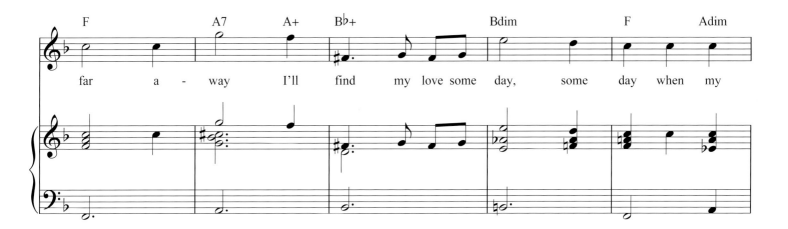

far a - way I'll find my love some day, some day when my

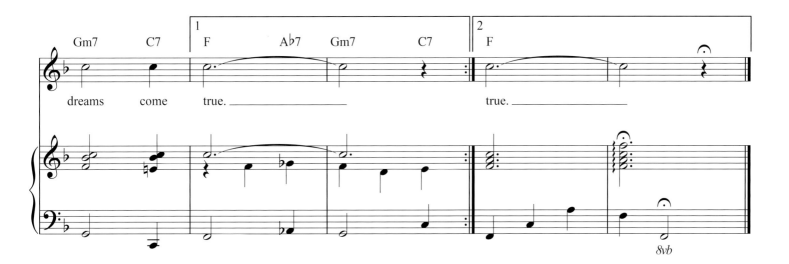

dreams come true. _____
true. _____

8vb

Whistle While You Work

From *SNOW WHITE AND THE SEVEN DWARFS*

Words by LARRY MOREY
Music by FRANK CHURCHILL

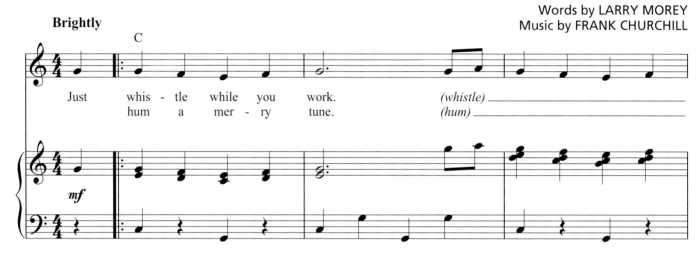

Brightly

Just whis-tle while you work. *(whistle)* _____
hum a mer-ry tune. *(hum)* _____

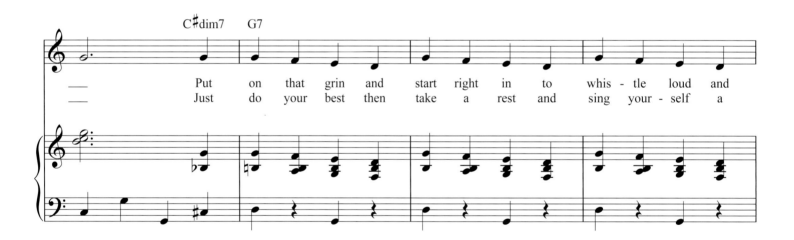

_____ Put on that grin and start right in to whis-tle loud and
_____ Just do your best then take a rest and sing your-self a

long. Just song. When there's too much to do, don't let it both-er

you. For - get your trou - ble, try to be just like a cheer - ful

chick - a - dee. And whis - tle while you work. *(whistle)* _____ Come

on, get smart, tune up and start to whis - tle while you work.

Give a Little Whistle

From *PINOCCHIO*

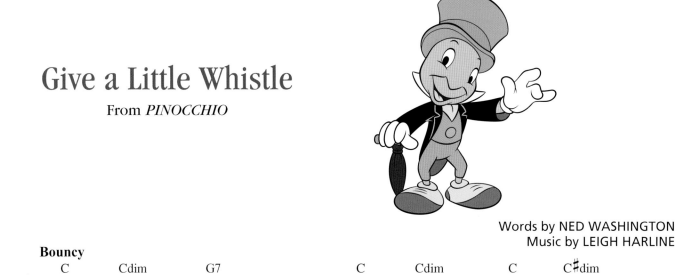

Words by NED WASHINGTON
Music by LEIGH HARLINE

When you get in trou-ble and you don't know right from wrong;
When you meet temp-ta-tion, and the urge is ver-y strong;
Give a lit-tle whis-tle! *(Whistle)* Give a lit-tle whis-tle! *(Whistle)*
Not just a lit-tle squeak; Puck-er up and

blow. And if your whis-tle's weak; yell, "Jim-i-ny

Crick-et." Take the straight and nar-row path And if you start to

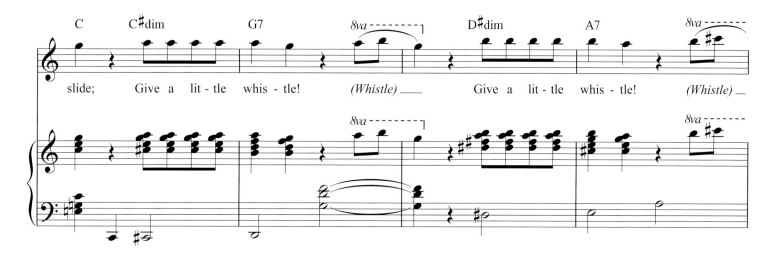

slide; Give a lit-tle whis-tle! *(Whistle)* ___ Give a lit-tle whis-tle! *(Whistle)* ___

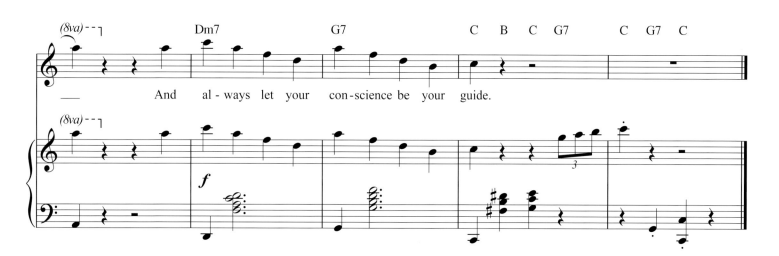

___ And al-ways let your con-science be your guide.

Hi-Diddle-Dee-Dee
(An Actor's Life for Me)
From *PINOCCHIO*

Words by NED WASHINGTON
Music by LEIGH HARLINE

Brightly

The grass is al - ways green - er in the oth - er fel - low's

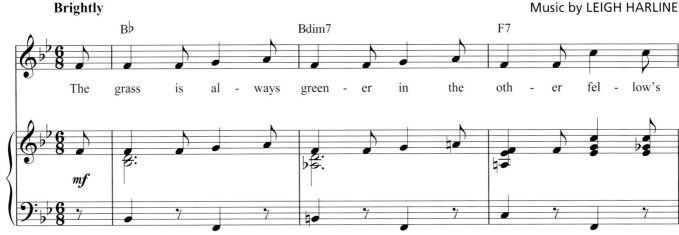

yard. No mat - ter what your life may be, you think your life is

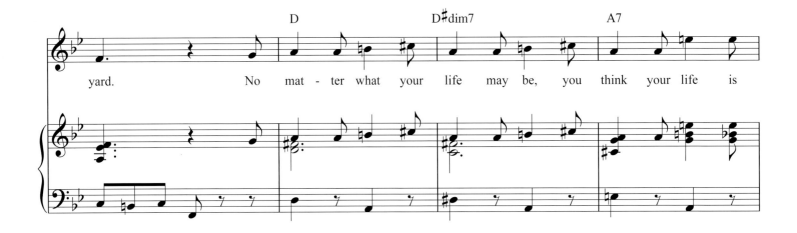

hard. If we could pick and choose, _____ and na - ture was - n't a

fac - tor, there's a bit of news:_____ I'd pick the life of an ac - tor.

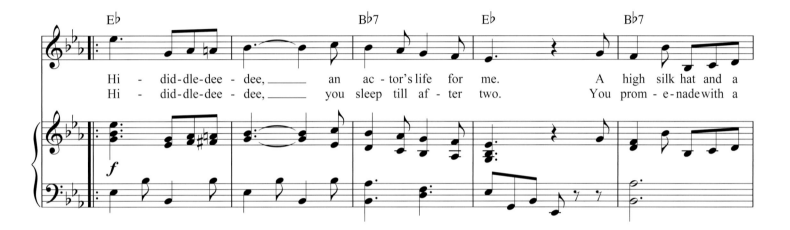

Hi - did-dle-dee - dee,_____ an ac - tor's life for me. A high silk hat and a
Hi - did-dle-dee - dee,_____ you sleep till af - ter two. You prom - e - nade with a

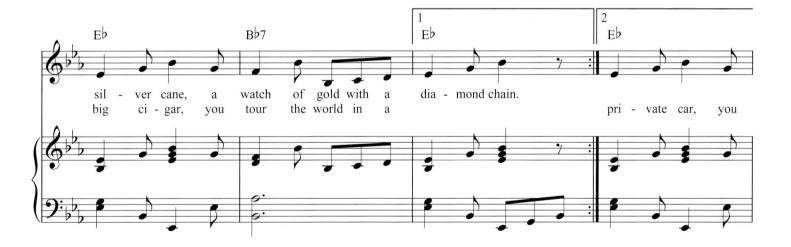

sil - ver cane, a watch of gold with a dia - mond chain.
big ci - gar, you tour the world in a pri - vate car, you

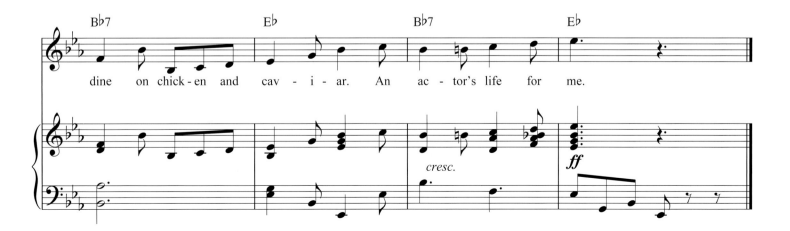

dine on chick - en and cav - i - ar. An ac - tor's life for me.

I've Got No Strings

From *PINOCCHIO*

Words by NED WASHINGTON
Music by LEIGH HARLINE

Joyfully

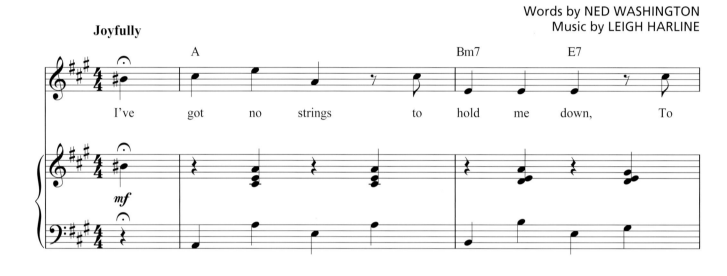

I've got no strings to hold me down, To

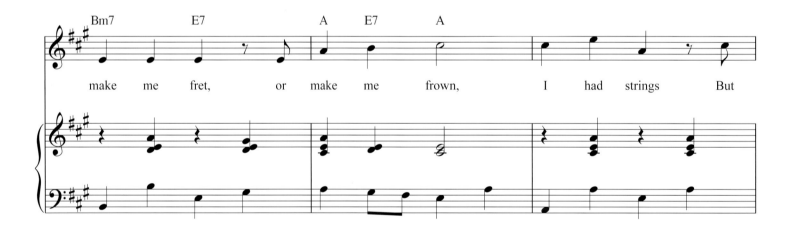

make me fret, or make me frown, I had strings But

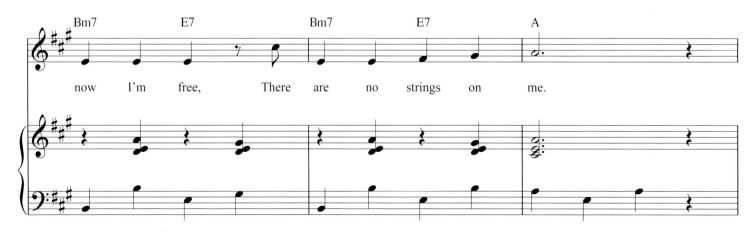

now I'm free, There are no strings on me.

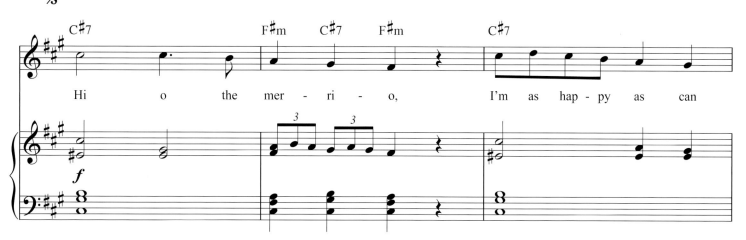

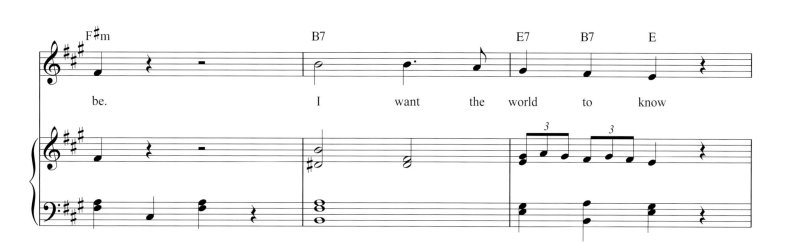

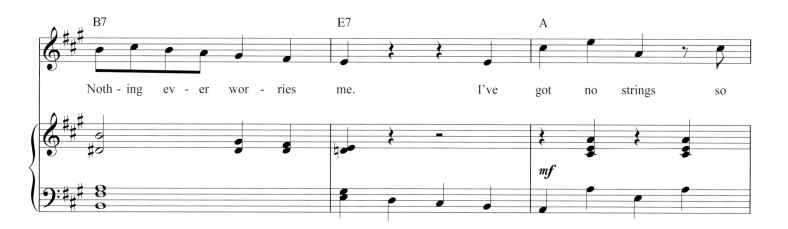

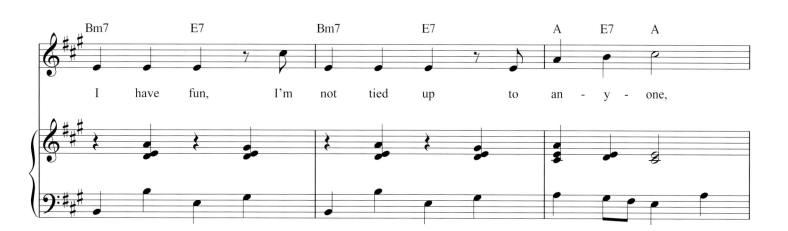

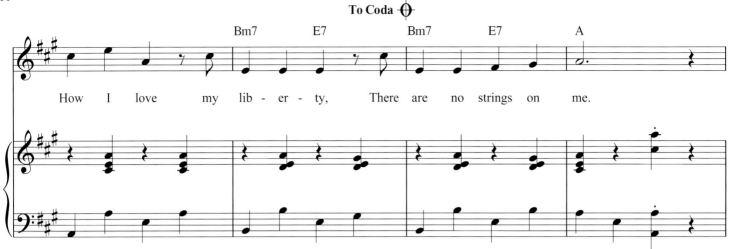

How I love my lib - er - ty, There are no strings on me.

(Instrumental interlude)

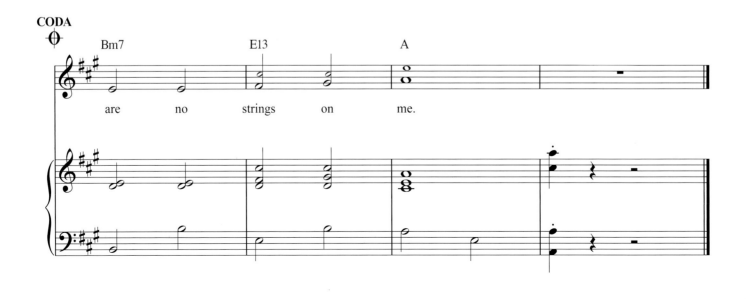

are no strings on me.

When You Wish Upon a Star

From *PINOCCHIO*

Words by NED WASHINGTON
Music by LEIGH HARLINE

With expression

When a star is born, they pos - sess a gift or two,

one of them is this: They have the pow - er ____ to make a wish come true.

When you wish up - on a star, makes no diff - 'rence

who you are, an-y-thing your heart de-sires will come to

you. If your heart is in your dream, no re-quest is

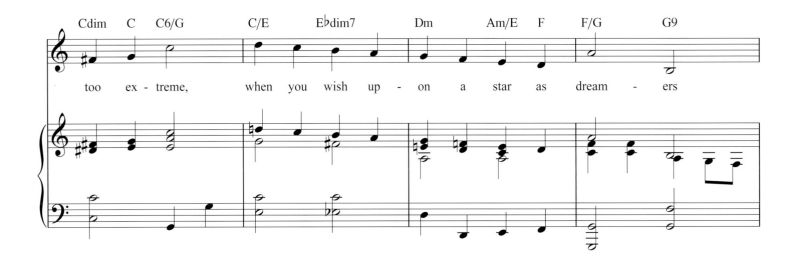

too ex-treme, when you wish up-on a star as dream-ers

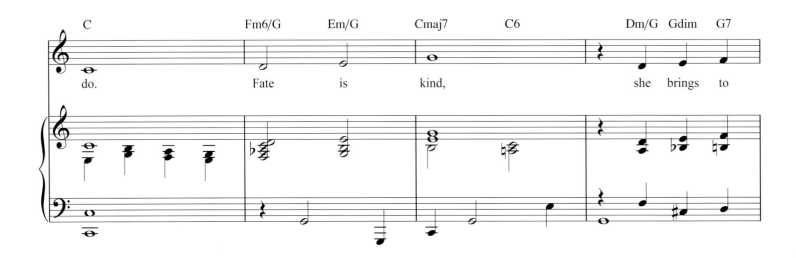

do. Fate is kind, she brings to

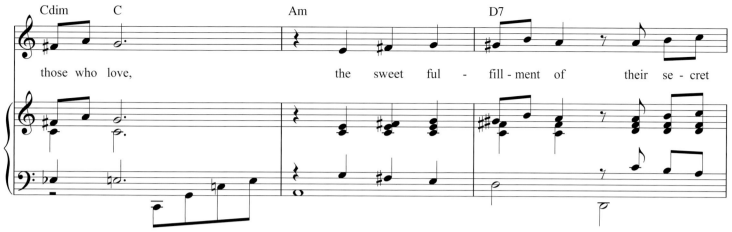

those who love, the sweet ful - fill - ment of their se - cret

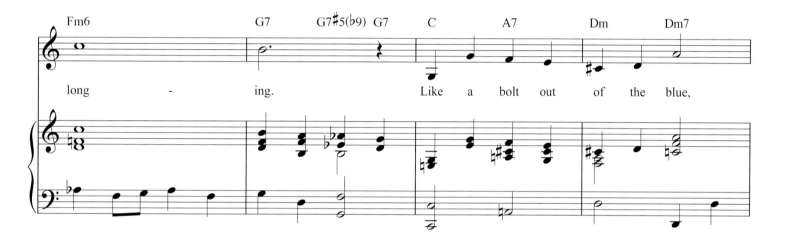

long - ing. Like a bolt out of the blue,

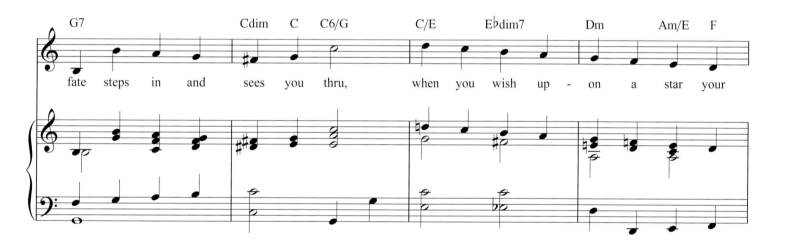

fate steps in and sees you thru, when you wish up - on a star your

dream comes true. dream comes true.

When I See an Elephant Fly

From *DUMBO*

Words by NED WASHINGTON
Music by OLIVER WALLACE

Moderately, in 2

I saw a pea-nut stand, _ heard a rub-ber band, _ I saw a nee-dle that winked _ its
front porch swing, _ heard a dia-mond ring, _ I saw a pol-ka-dot rail - road

eye. }
tie. }
But I think I will have seen ev-'ry-thing _ when I see an el-e-phant

fly. I saw a fly.

I e-ven heard _ a choc-o-late drop, _ I

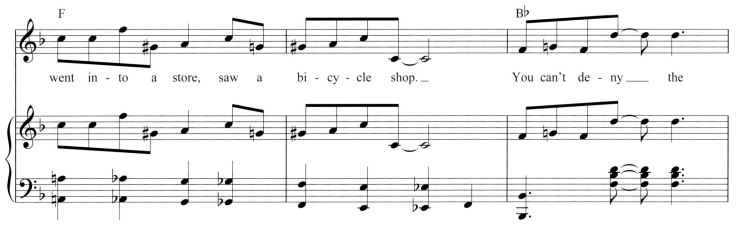

went in - to a store, saw a bi - cy - cle shop. __ You can't de - ny __ the

things that you see, __ but I know there's cer - tain things that just can't be. __ The oth - er

day, by chance, __ saw an old barn dance, __ and I just laughed till I thought __ I'd die. But I

think I will have seen ev - 'ry - thing __ when I see an el - e - phant fly.

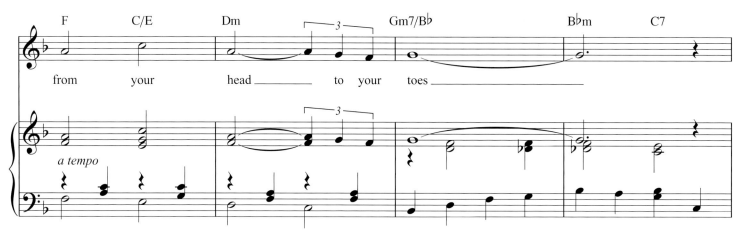

from your head _____ to your toes _____

you're not much, _____ good-ness knows, _____

but you're so pre-cious to me, cute as can be, ba-by of

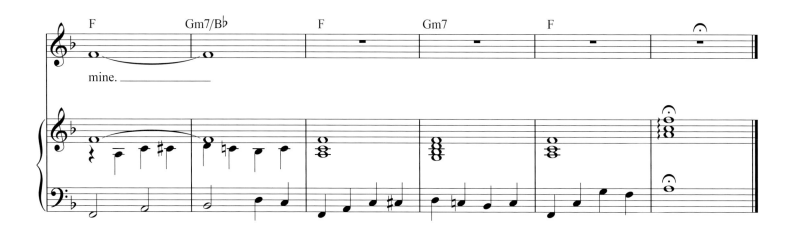

mine. _____

Lavender Blue
(Dilly Dilly)

From *SO DEAR TO MY HEART*

Words by LARRY MOREY
Music by ELIOT DANIEL

Moderately

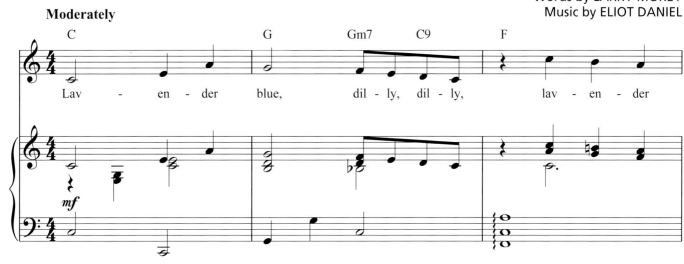

Lav - en - der blue, dil - ly, dil - ly, lav - en - der

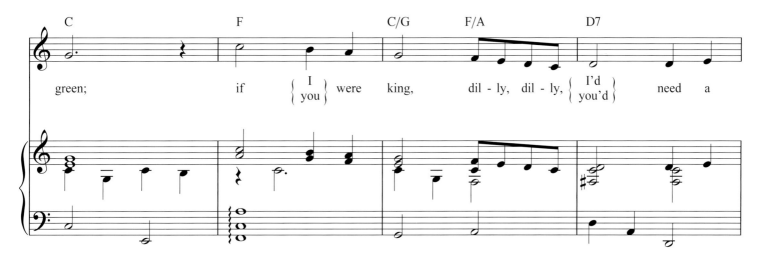

green; if { I / you } were king, dil - ly, dil - ly, { I'd / you'd } need a

queen. Who told me so, dil - ly, dil - ly, who told me

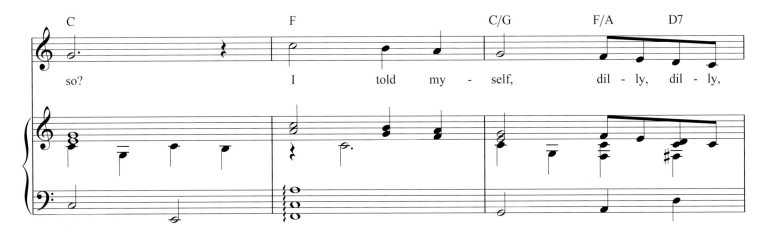

so? I told my-self, dil - ly, dil - ly,

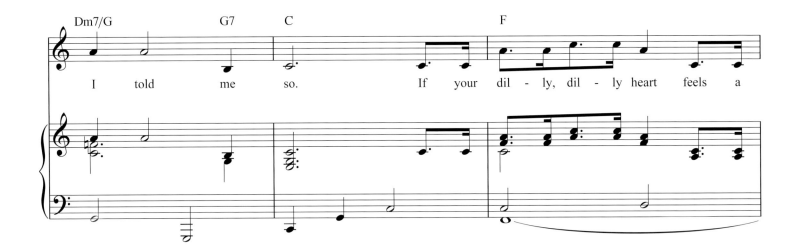

I told me so. If your dil - ly, dil - ly heart feels a

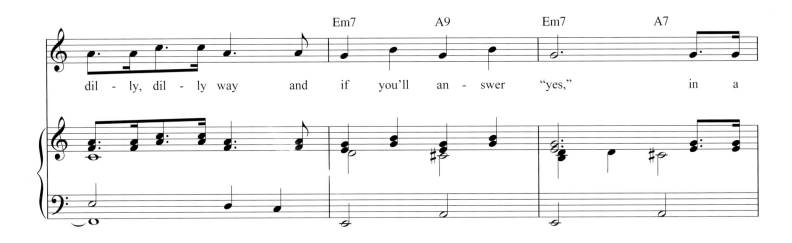

dil - ly, dil - ly way and if you'll an - swer "yes," in a

pret - ty lit - tle church on a dil - ly, dil - ly day {you'll / I'll} be wed in a

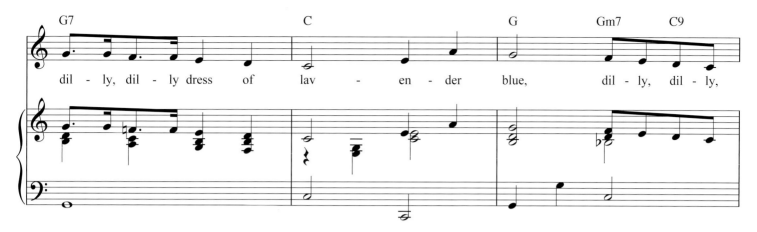

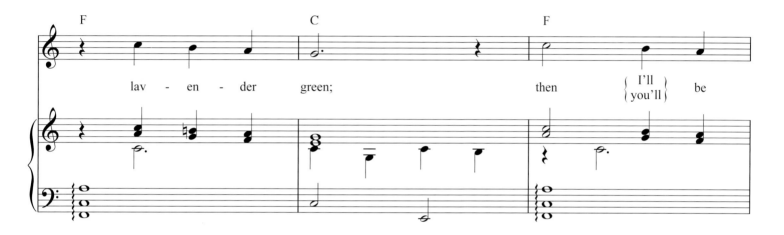

Little April Shower

From *BAMBI*

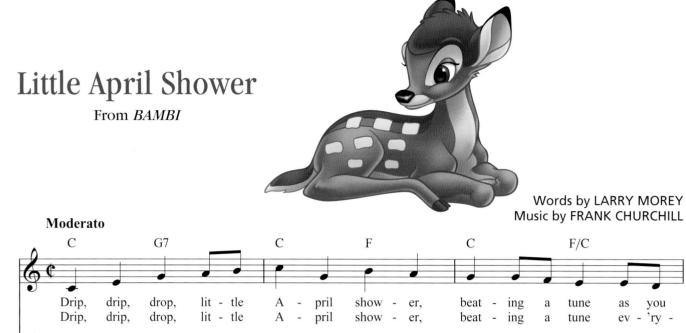

Words by LARRY MOREY
Music by FRANK CHURCHILL

Moderato

Drip, drip, drop, lit-tle A-pril show-er, beat-ing a tune as you
Drip, drip, drop, lit-tle A-pril show-er, beat-ing a tune ev-'ry-

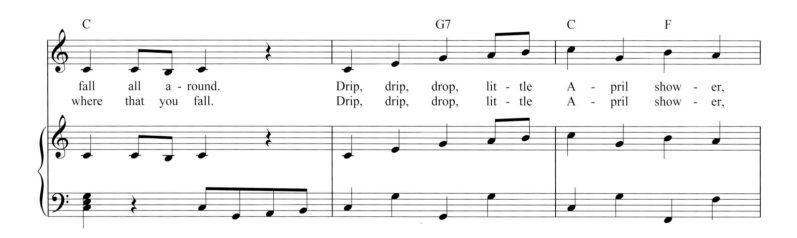

fall all a-round. Drip, drip, drop, lit-tle A-pril show-er,
where that you fall. Drip, drip, drop, lit-tle A-pril show-er,

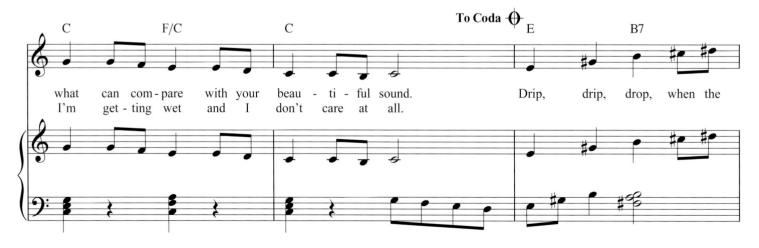

what can com-pare with your beau-ti-ful sound. Drip, drip, drop, when the
I'm get-ting wet and I don't care at all.

sky is cloud - y your pret - ty mu - sic can bright - en the day.

D.C. al Coda

Drip, drip, drop, when the sun says, "How - dy" you say "Good - bye" right a - way. _____

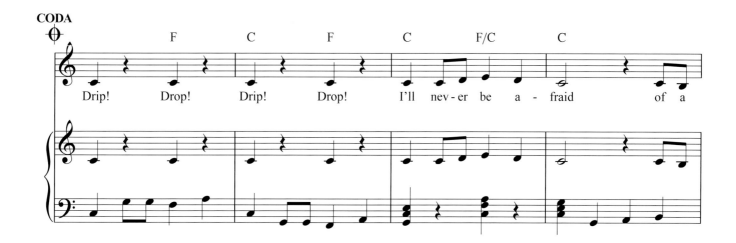

CODA

Drip! Drop! Drip! Drop! I'll nev - er be a - fraid of a

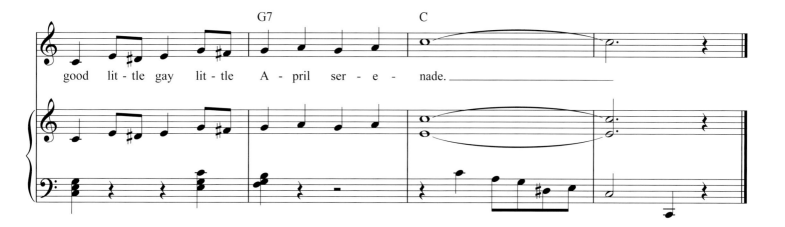

good lit - tle gay lit - tle A - pril ser - e - nade. _____

Zip-A-Dee-Doo-Dah

From *SONG OF THE SOUTH*

Words by RAY GILBERT
Music by ALLIE WRUBEL

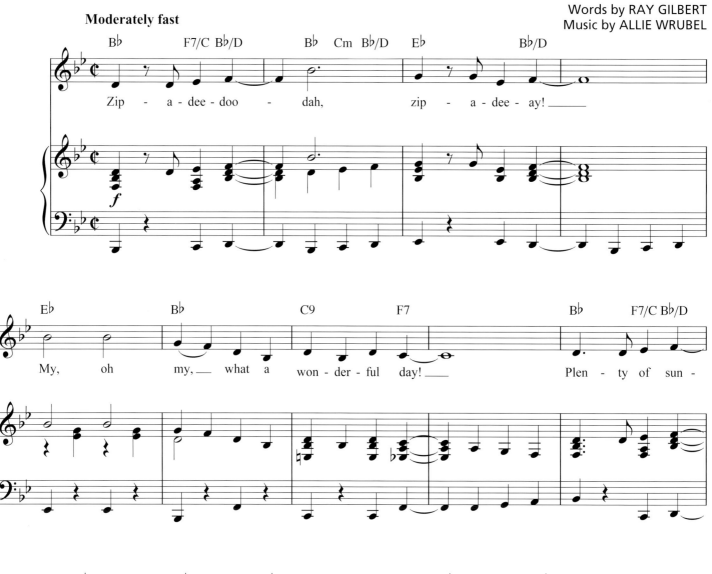

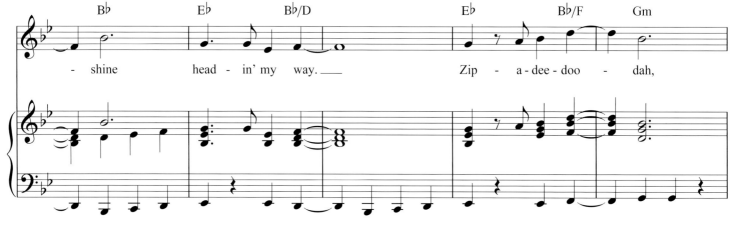

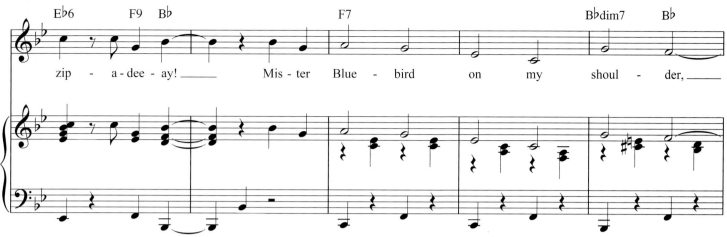

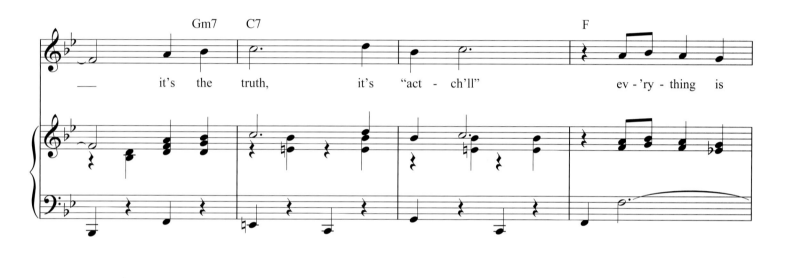

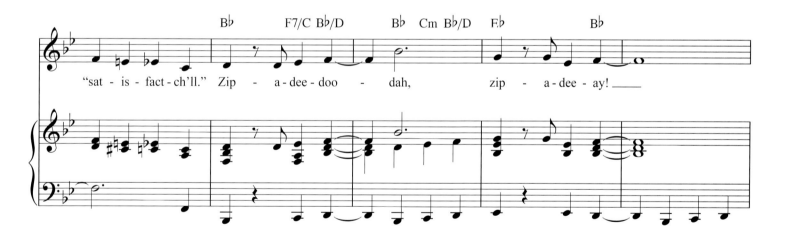

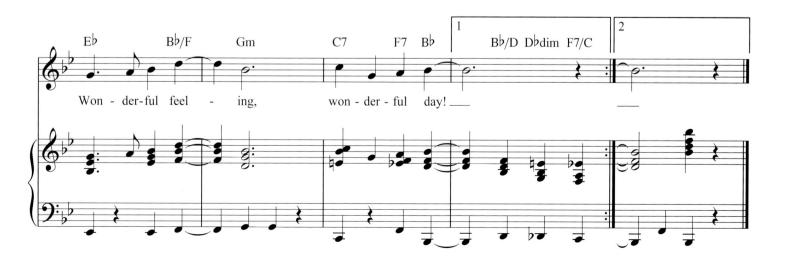

Bibbidi-Bobbidi-Boo
(The Magic Song)
From *CINDERELLA*

Words by JERRY LIVINGSTON
Music by MACK DAVID and AL HOFFMAN

Brightly

Sa - la - ga - doo - la men-chic-ka boo - la bib - bi - di - bob - bi - di - boo.

Put 'em to - geth - er and what have you got bib - bi - di - bob - bi - di - boo.

Sa - la - ga - doo - la men-chic-ka boo - la bib-bi-di-bob-bi-di-boo. It -'ll do mag-ic be-lieve it or not,

A Dream Is a Wish Your Heart Makes

From *CINDERELLA*

Words and Music by MACK DAVID,
AL HOFFMAN and JERRY LIVINGSTON

Moderately

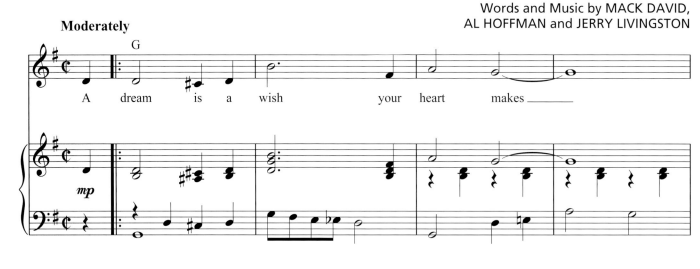

A dream is a wish your heart makes _____

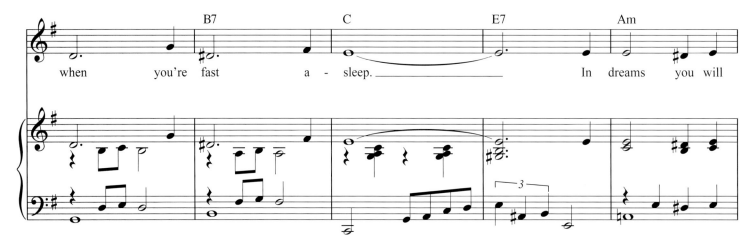

when you're fast a - sleep. _____ In dreams you will

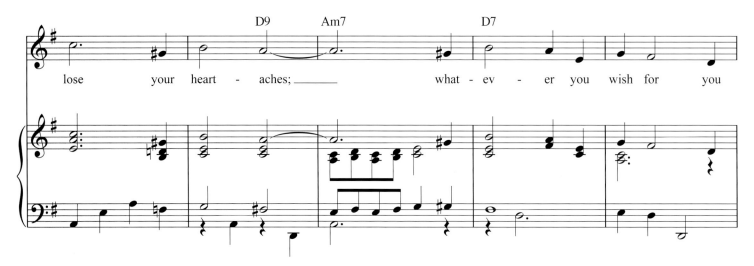

lose your heart - aches; _____ what - ev - er you wish for you

I'm Late

From *ALICE IN WONDERLAND*

Words by BOB HILLIARD
Music by SAMMY FAIN

Brightly

I'm late, I'm late for a ver-y im-por-tant date. No time to say hel - lo, good-bye, I'm late, I'm late, I'm late, I'm late, and when I wave, I lose the time I save. My fuzz-y ears and

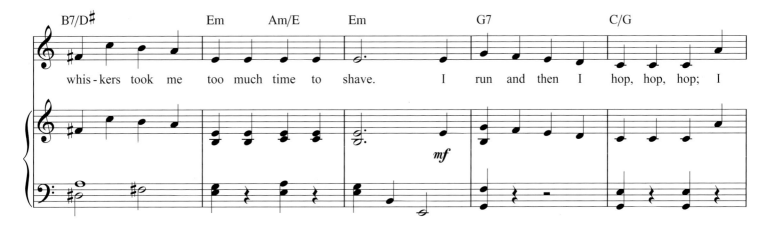

whis-kers took me too much time to shave. I run and then I hop, hop, hop; I

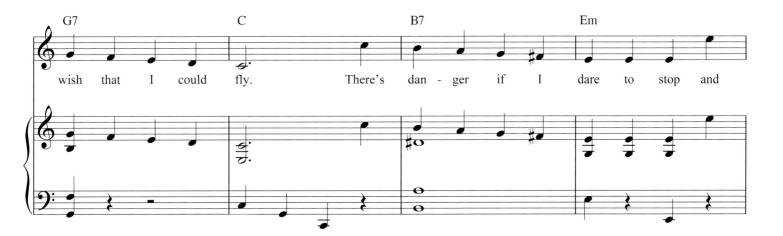

wish that I could fly. There's dan - ger if I dare to stop and

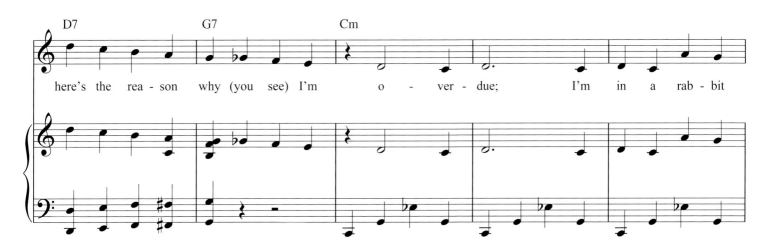

here's the rea - son why (you see) I'm o - ver-due; I'm in a rab - bit

stew. Can't e - ven say good - bye, hel - lo, I'm late, I'm late, I'm late.

The Second Star to the Right

From *PETER PAN*

Words by SAMMY CAHN
Music by SAMMY FAIN

Moderately slow

The sec-ond star to the right shines in the night for you,

to tell you that the dreams you plan real-ly can come true.

The sec-ond star to the right shines with a light that's rare; and if it's Nev-er-

You Can Fly! You Can Fly! You Can Fly!

From *PETER PAN*

Words by SAMMY CAHN
Music by SAMMY FAIN

Moderately slow

Think of the pres-ents you're brought, an-y mer-ry lit-tle thought.

Think of Christ-mas, think of snow, think of sleigh bells, here we go! Like

rein-deer in the sky. _____ You can fly! You can

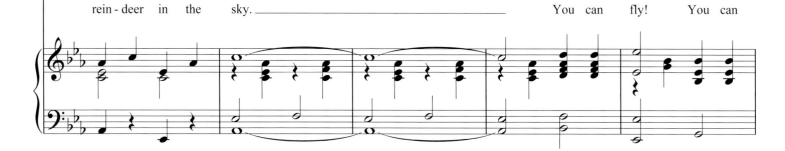

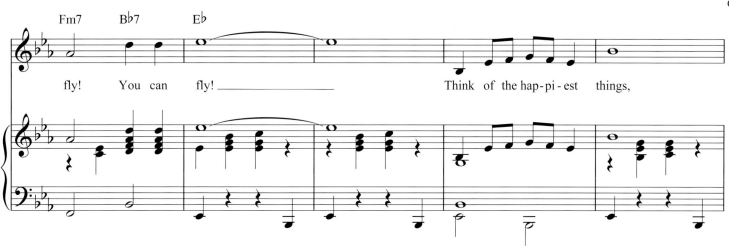

fly! You can fly! _____ Think of the hap-pi-est things,

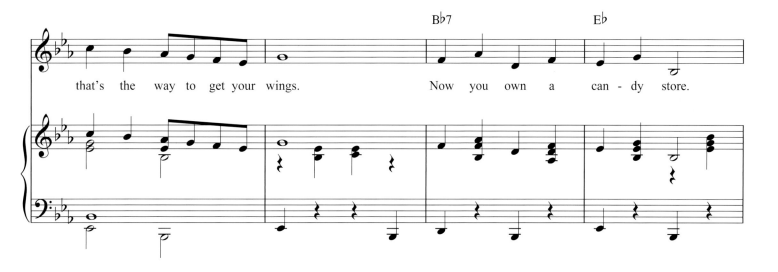

that's the way to get your wings. Now you own a can-dy store.

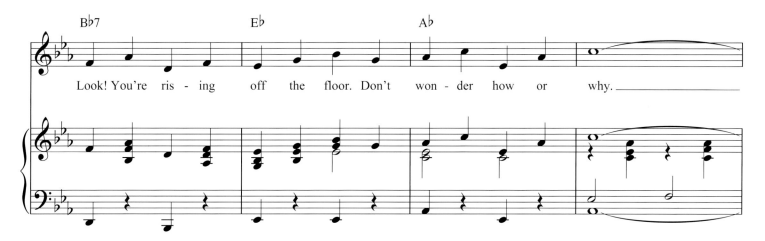

Look! You're ris-ing off the floor. Don't won-der how or why. _____

_____ You can fly! You can fly! You can fly! _____

Soon you'll zoom all a-round the room, all it takes is faith and

trust. But the thing that's a pos-i-tive must is a lit-tle bit of Pix-ie

Dust. The dust is a pos-i-tive must! _____

When there's a smile in your heart there's no bet-ter time to start.

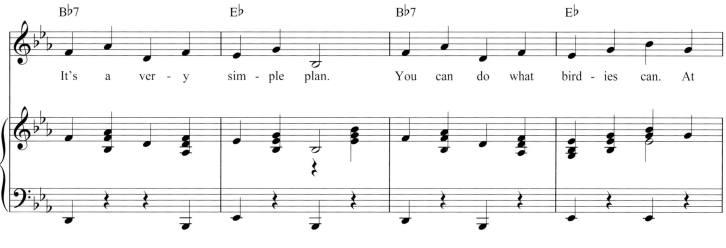

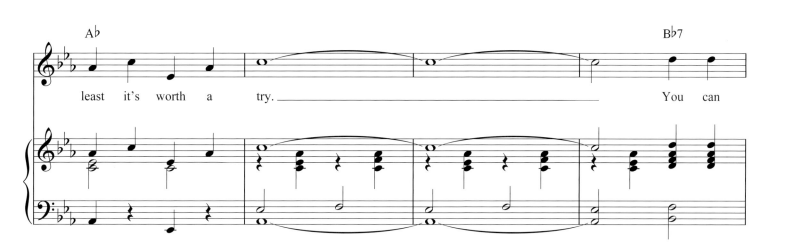

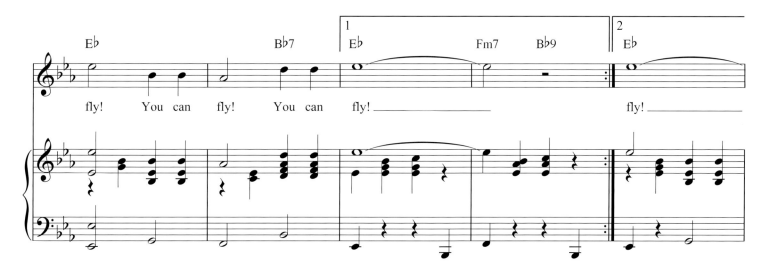

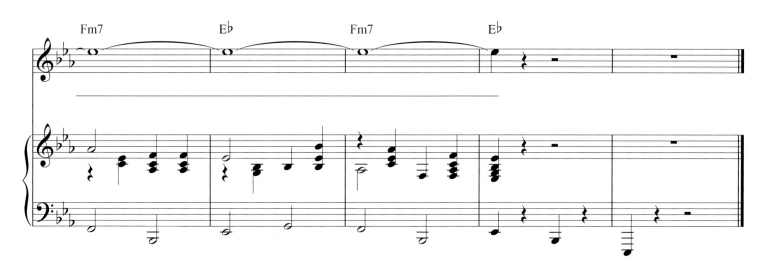

Bella Notte
(This Is the Night)

From *LADY AND THE TRAMP*

Music and Lyrics by PEGGY LEE
and SONNY BURKE

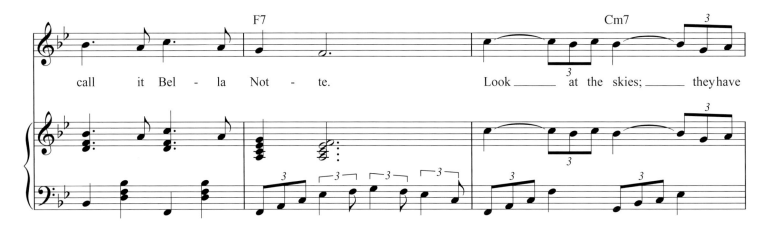

take this love ___ of your loved one, you'll need it a-bout this
Side by side ___ with your loved one you'll find en - chant - ment

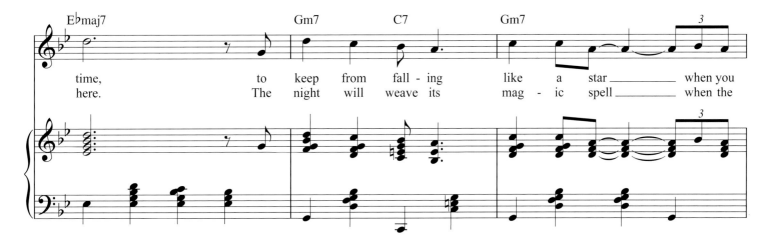

time, to keep from fall - ing like a star ___ when you
here. The night will weave its mag - ic spell ___ when the

make that diz - zy climb.}
one you love is near.}
For this ___ is the night ___ and the

heav-ens are right ___ on this love - ly Bel - la Not - te.

Once Upon A Dream

From *SLEEPING BEAUTY*

Words and Music by SAMMY FAIN
and JACK LAWRENCE
Adapted from a Theme by TCHAIKOVSKY

Moderately

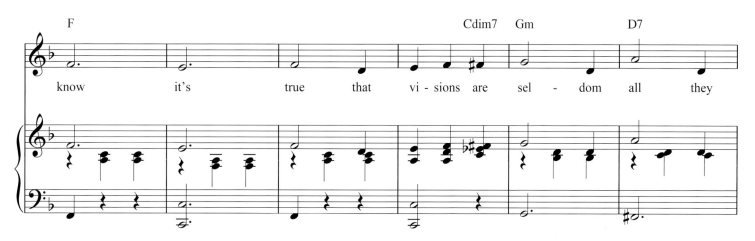

know   it's   true   that   vi - sions are   sel - dom   all   they

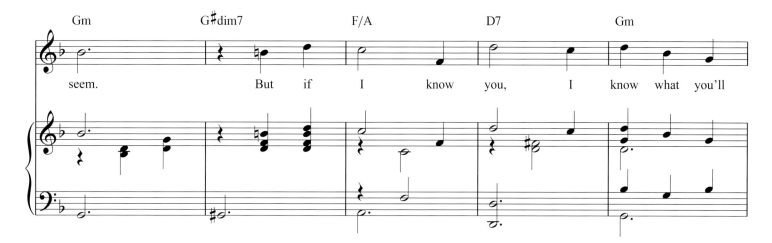

seem.   But   if   I   know   you,   I   know   what   you'll

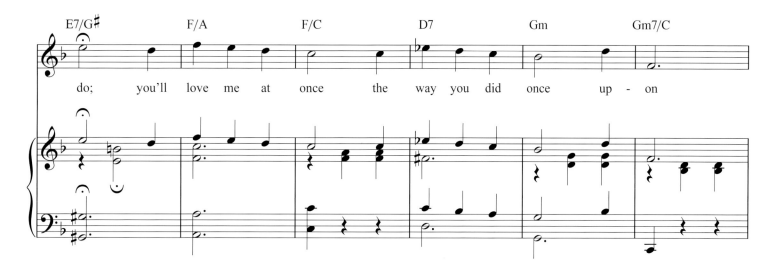

do;   you'll   love   me   at   once   the   way   you   did   once   up - on

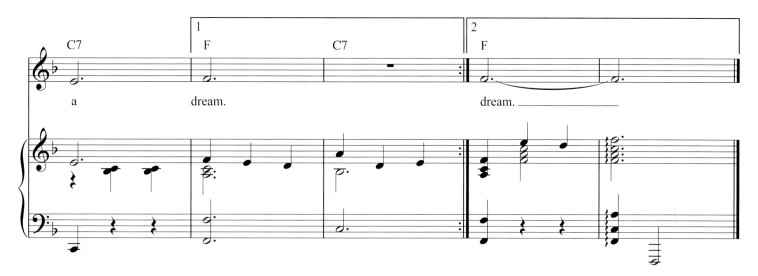

a   dream.   dream.

Cruella De Vil

From *101 DALMATIANS*

Words and Music by
MEL LEVEN

Cru - el - la De Vil, __ Cru - el - la De Vil, __ if she does-n't scare __ you, no

e - vil thing will. __ To see her is to take a sud - den chill. __ Cru -

el - la, Cru - el - la De Vil. ____ The curl of her lips, __ the

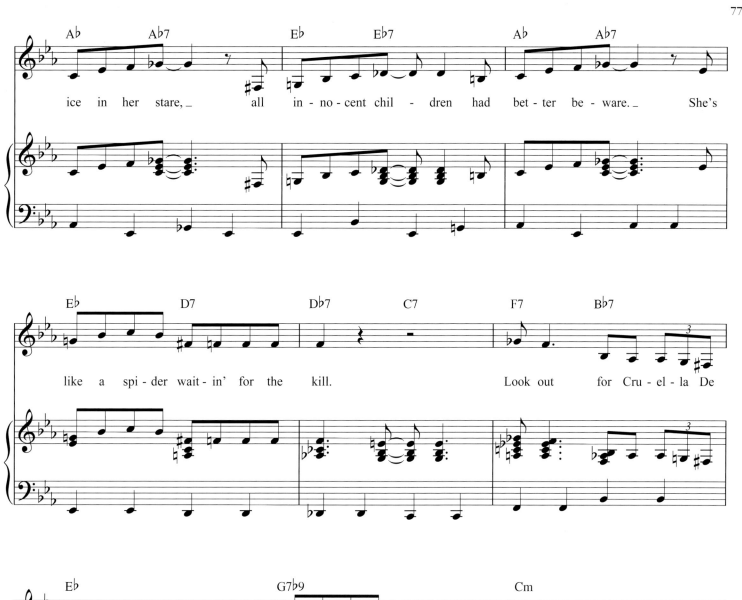

ice in her stare, _ all in - no - cent chil - dren had bet - ter be - ware. _ She's

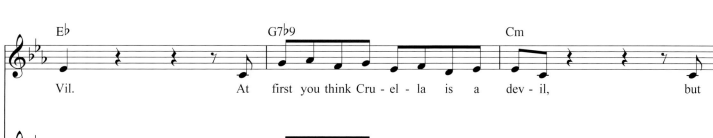

like a spi - der wait - in' for the kill. Look out for Cru - el - la De

Vil. At first you think Cru - el - la is a dev - il, but

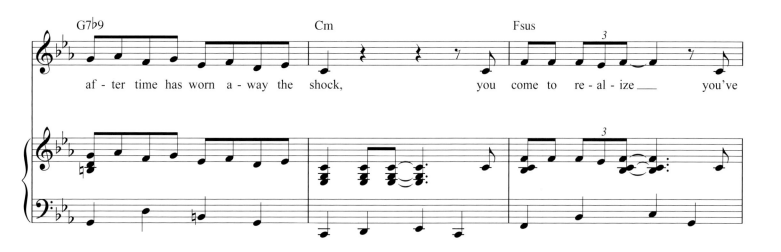

af - ter time has worn a - way the shock, you come to re - al - ize _ you've

seen her kind of eyes _ watch-ing you from un-der-neath a rock. This

vam - pi - re bat, __ this in - hu - man beast, __ she ought to be locked _ up and

nev - er re - leased. _ The world was such a whole - some place un - til ___ Cru -

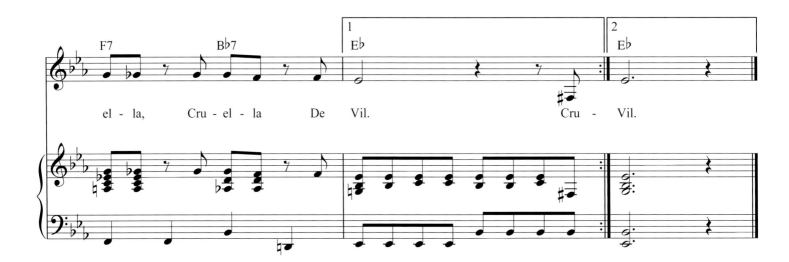

el - la, Cru - el - la De Vil. Cru - Vil.

The Bare Necessities

From *THE JUNGLE BOOK*

Words and Music by
TERRY GILKYSON

Brightly

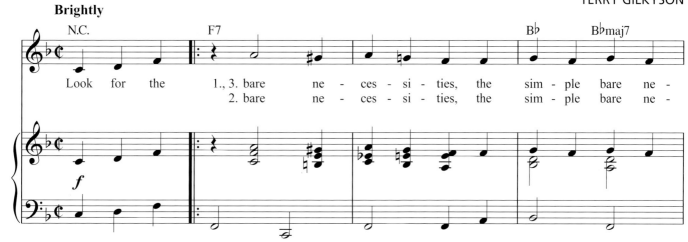

Look for the 1., 3. bare ne - ces - si - ties, the sim - ple bare ne -
2. bare ne - ces - si - ties, the sim - ple bare ne -

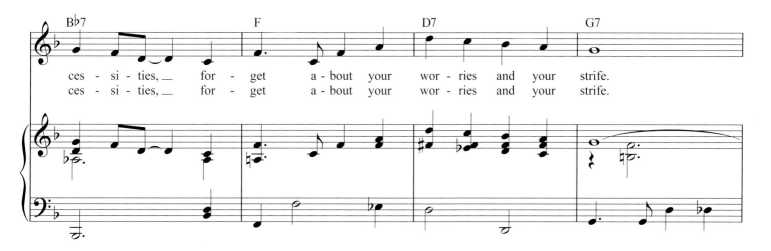

ces - si - ties,___ for - get a - bout your wor - ries and your strife.
ces - si - ties,___ for - get a - bout your wor - ries and your strife.

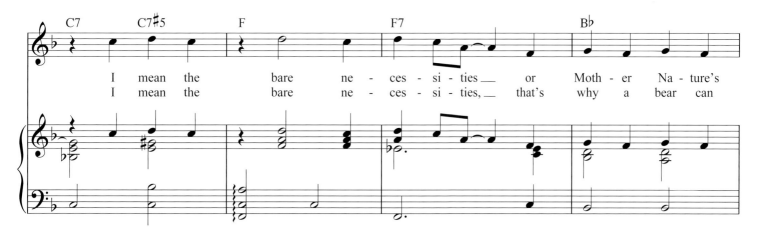

I mean the bare ne - ces - si - ties___ or Moth - er Na - ture's
I mean the bare ne - ces - si - ties,___ that's why a bear can

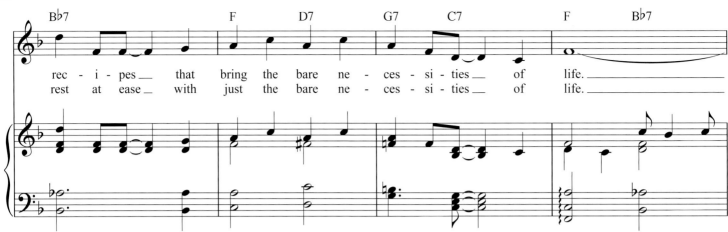

recipes that bring the bare necessities of life.
rest at ease with just the bare necessities of life.

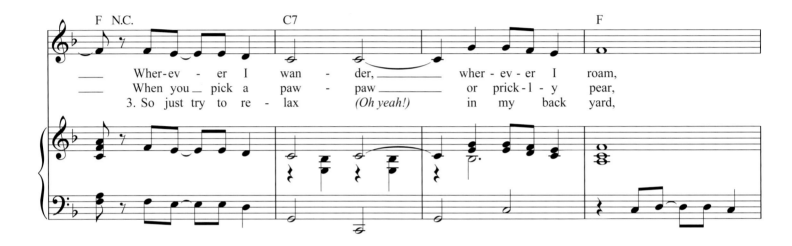

Wherever I wander, wherever I roam,
When you pick a pawpaw or prickly pear,
3. So just try to relax *(Oh yeah!)* in my back yard,

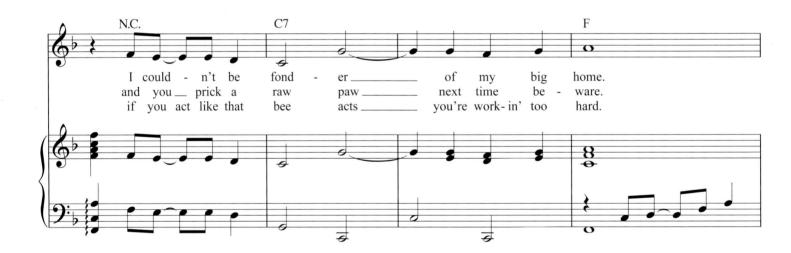

I couldn't be fonder of my big home.
and you prick a raw paw next time beware.
if you act like that bee acts you're workin' too hard.

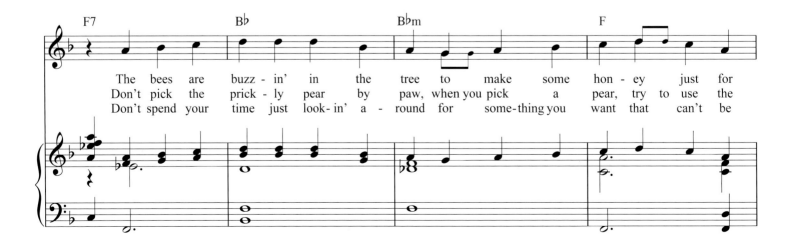

The bees are buzzin' in the tree to make some honey just for
Don't pick the prickly pear by paw, when you pick a pear, try to use the
Don't spend your time just lookin' around for something you want that can't be

A Spoonful of Sugar

From *MARY POPPINS*

Words and Music by RICHARD M. SHERMAN
and ROBERT B. SHERMAN

Brightly

very clear to see that a
move the job a-long for a } spoon-ful of sug-ar helps the med-i-cine go
task is not a grind. for a

down, the med-i-cine go dow-wown, med-i-cine go down. Just a

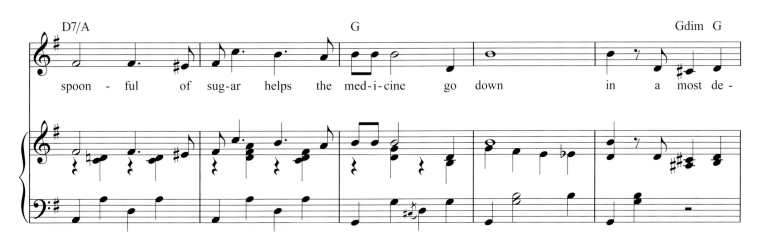

spoon-ful of sug-ar helps the med-i-cine go down in a most de-

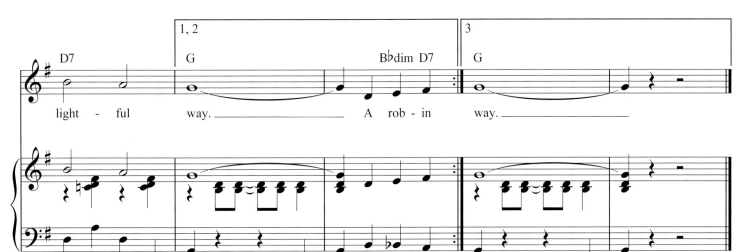

light - ful way. A rob-in way.

Supercalifragilistic-
expialidocious

From *MARY POPPINS*

Words and Music by RICHARD M. SHERMAN
and ROBERT B. SHERMAN

Brightly

Mary Poppins:

C   Cmaj7   C6   C♯dim7   G7

Su - per - cal - i - frag - il - is - tic - ex - pi - al - i - do - cious!

Dm7   G7   Dm7   G7   C

E - ven though the sound of it is some - thing quite a - tro - cious,

Cmaj7   C7   F

if you say it loud e - nough, you'll al - ways sound pre - co - cious.

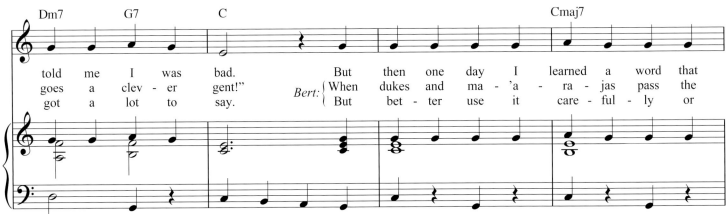

told me I was bad.
goes a clev - er gent!"
got a lot to say.

Bert: { When dukes and ma - 'a - ra - jas pass the
But bet - ter use it care - ful - ly or

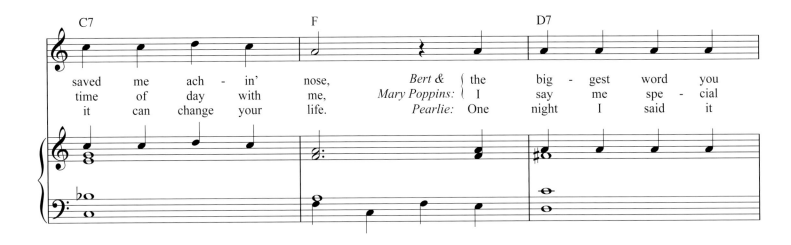

saved me ach - in' nose,
time of day with me,
it can change your life.

Bert & Mary Poppins: { the big - gest word you
I say me word spe - cial
Pearlie: One night I said it

ev - er 'eard and this is 'ow it goes: Oh! }
word and then they ask me out to tea. *All:* Oh! }
to me girl and ask now me girl's me wife. *All:* She's

Su - per - cal - i -
Su - per - cal - i -

frag - il - is - tic - ex - pi - al - i - do - cious! E - ven though the
frag - il - is - tic - ex - pi - al - i - do - cious! Su - per - cal - i -

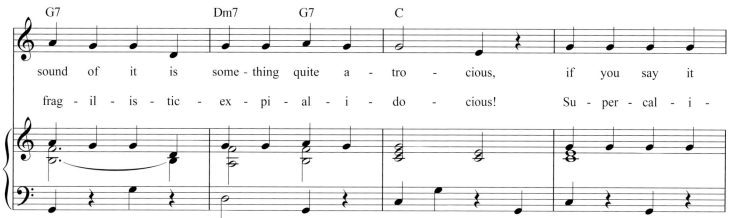

sound of it is some-thing quite a-tro - cious, if you say it
frag - il - is - tic - ex - pi - al - i - do - cious! Su - per - cal - i -

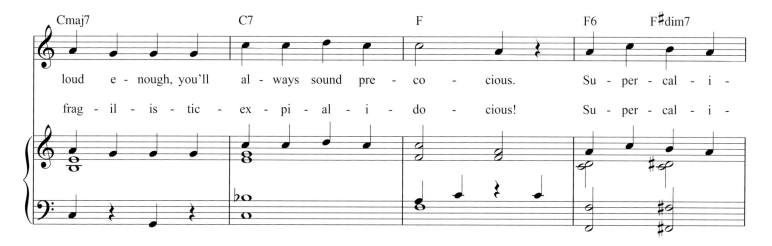

loud e - nough, you'll al - ways sound pre - co - cious. Su - per - cal - i -
frag - il - is - tic - ex - pi - al - i - do - cious! Su - per - cal - i -

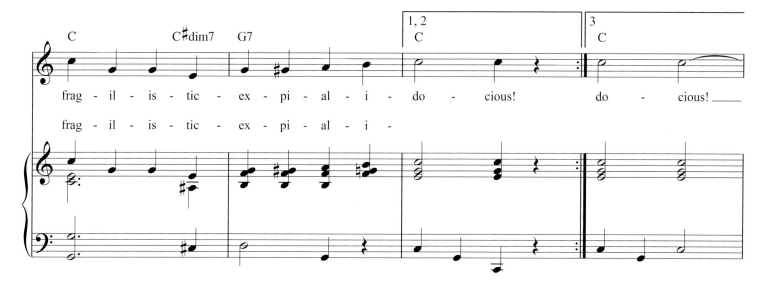

frag - il - is - tic - ex - pi - al - i - do - cious! do - cious! _____
frag - il - is - tic - ex - pi - al - i -

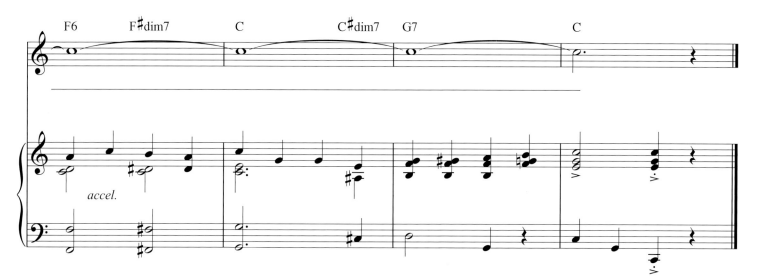

accel.

Ev'rybody Wants to Be a Cat

From *THE ARISTOCATS*

Words by FLOYD HUDDLESTON
Music by AL RINKER

Easy Swing

Ev - 'ry - bod - y wants to be a cat, be-cause a cat's the on - ly cat who

knows where it's at! ___ Ev - 'ry - bod - y's pick-in' up on that fe - line beat, ___

'cause ev - 'ry-thing else is ob - so - lete. A square with a horn ___ makes you wish you weren't born ___ ev - 'ry

Eb

time he plays! _ But with a square in the act, _ you can set mu-sic back _ to the

Dm7b5   G7   Fm7b5   G7

Cm   Dm7b5   G7   Cm   Cm(maj7)   Cm7   Cm6

cave-man days! _

I've heard some corn-y birds who tried to sing,   but still a
Ev - 'ry - bod-y wants to be a cat,   be-cause a

Ab   Fm   D7   G7   Cm   Cm(maj7)

cat's the on - ly cat who knows how to swing! _ Who wants to dig a long-haired gig and
cat's the on - ly cat who knows where it's at! ____ When play-ing jazz you al - ways has a

Cm7   Cm6   Ab   Dm7b5   1. Cm/G Gm   Cm   2. Cm/G Gm   Cm

stuff like that, _ when ev-'ry-bod-y wants to be a cat? _ A
wel - come mat, _ 'cause ev-'ry-bod-y digs a swing-ing cat! _

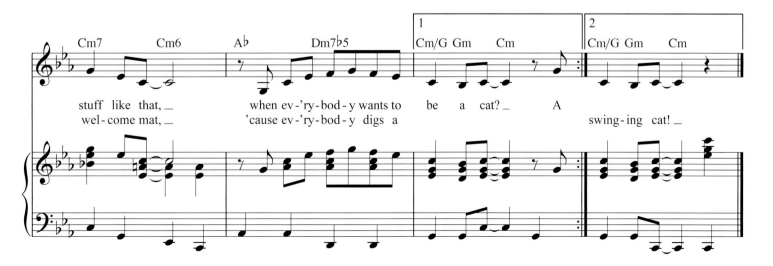

Winnie the Pooh

From *THE MANY ADVENTURES OF WINNIE THE POOH*

Words and Music by RICHARD M. SHERMAN
and ROBERT B. SHERMAN

Lyrics:
Win-nie the Pooh, Win-nie the Pooh. Tub-by lit-tle cub-by all stuffed with fluff. He's Win-nie the Pooh, Win-nie the Pooh. Wil-ly nil-ly sil-ly ole bear. Deep in the hun-dred a-cre wood where Chris-to-pher Rob-in plays,

The Wonderful Thing About Tiggers

From *THE MANY ADVENTURES OF WINNIE THE POOH*

Words and Music by RICHARD M. SHERMAN
and ROBERT B. SHERMAN

Very brightly

The won-der-ful thing a-bout tig-gers___ is tig-gers are won-der-ful
won-der-ful thing a-bout tig-gers___ is tig-gers are won-der-ful

things! Their tops are made out of rub-ber;___ their bot-toms are made out of
chaps! They're load-ed with vim and with vig-or;___ they love to leap in your

springs! They're bounc-y, trounc-y, flounc-y, pounc-y, Fun! Fun! Fun! Fun!
laps! They're jump-y, bump-y, clump-y, thump-y, Fun! Fun! Fun! Fun!

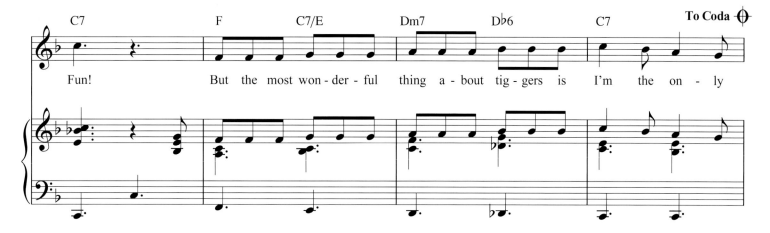

Fun! But the most won-der-ful thing a-bout tig-gers is I'm the on-ly

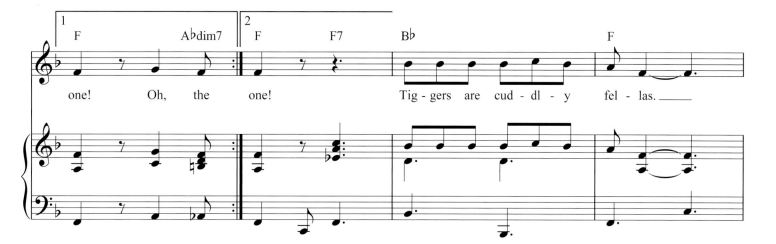

one! Oh, the one! Tig-gers are cud-dl-y fel-las.____

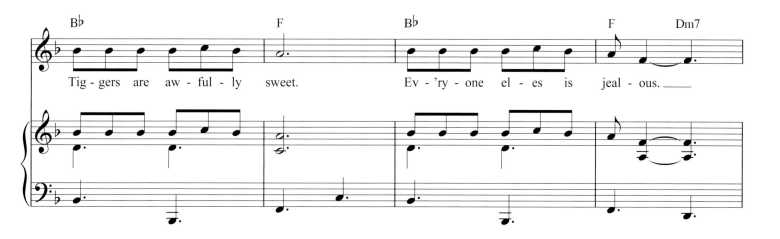

Tig-gers are aw-ful-ly sweet. Ev-'ry-one el-es is jeal-ous.____

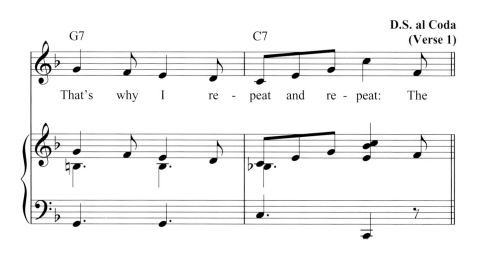

That's why I re-peat and re-peat: The

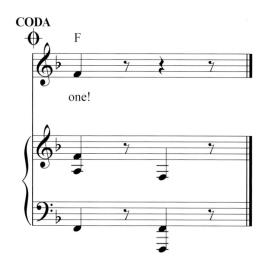

one!

Candle on the Water

From *PETE'S DRAGON*

Words and Music by AL KASHA
and JOEL HIRSCHHORN

A cold and friend-less tide has found you, don't let the storm-y dark-ness

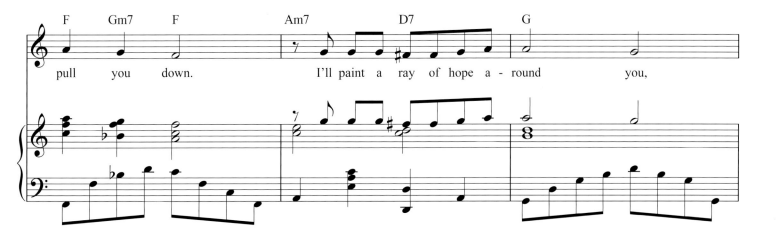

pull you down. I'll paint a ray of hope a-round you,

cir-cling in the air light-ed by a prayer. _____

I'll be your can-dle on the wa-ter, this flame in-side of me will

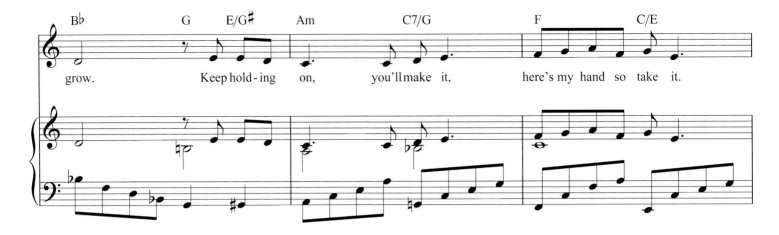

grow. Keep hold-ing on, you'll make it, here's my hand so take it.

Look for me reach-ing out to show as sure as riv-ers flow, I'll nev-er let you

go, I'll nev-er let you go, I'll nev-er let you

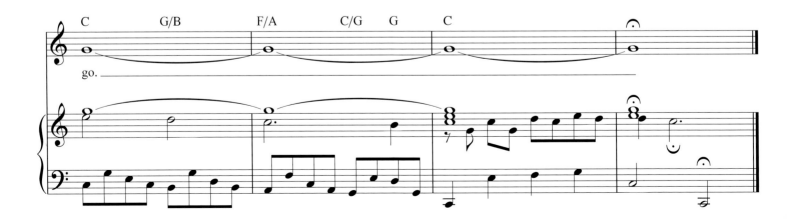

go.

Part of Your World

From *THE LITTLE MERMAID*

Music by ALAN MENKEN
Lyrics by HOWARD ASHMAN

Moderately bright

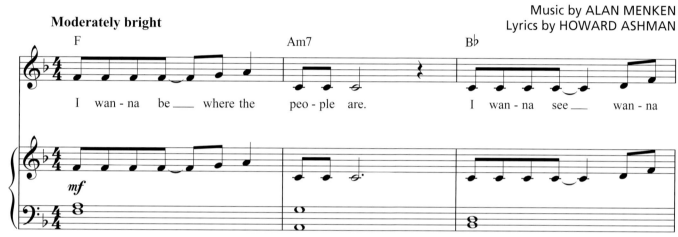

I wan-na be where the peo-ple are. I wan-na see wan-na

see 'em danc-in', walk-in' a-round on those, what-d'-ya call 'em, oh,

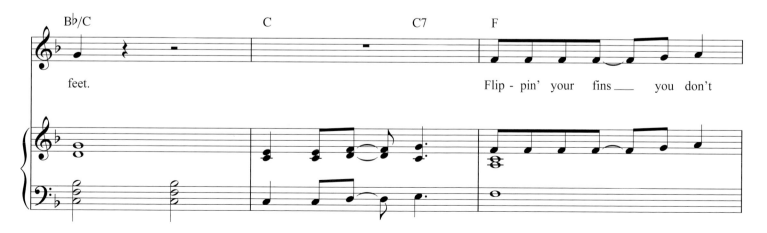

feet. Flip-pin' your fins you don't

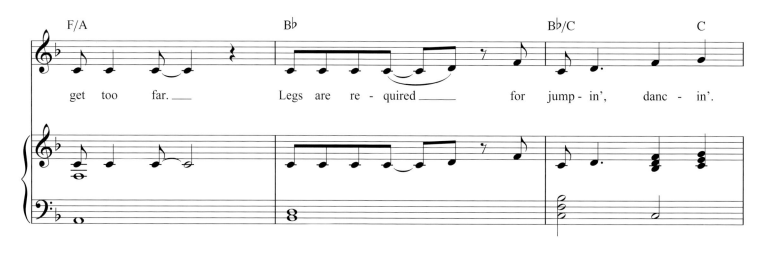

get too far.___ Legs are re - quired ___ for jump - in', danc - in'.

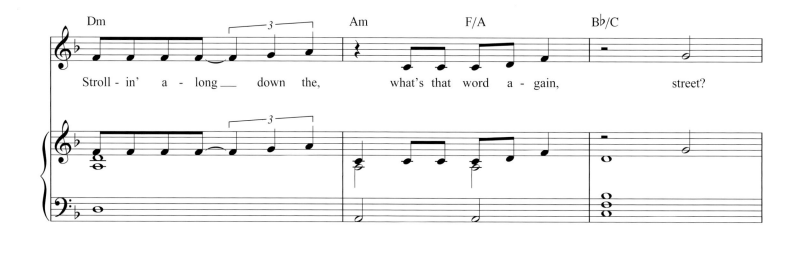

Stroll - in' a - long ___ down the, what's that word a - gain, street?

Up where they walk, up where they run, up where they

stay all day ___ in the sun. ___ Wan - der - in' free, wish I could

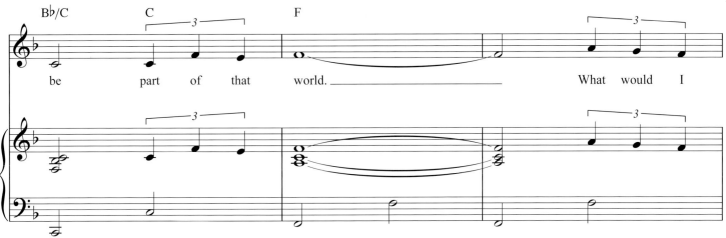

be part of that world. _____ What would I

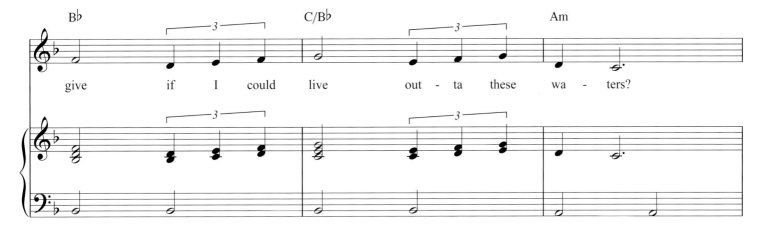

give if I could live out - ta these wa - ters?

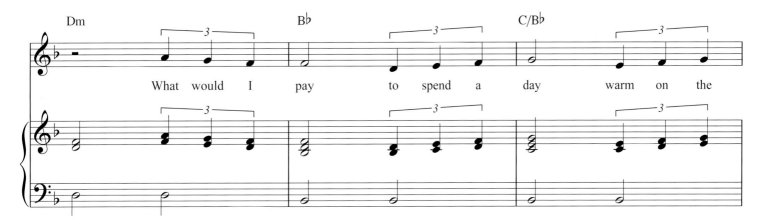

What would I pay to spend a day warm on the

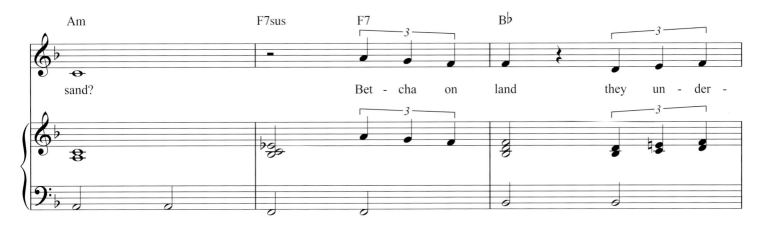

sand? Bet - cha on land they un - der -

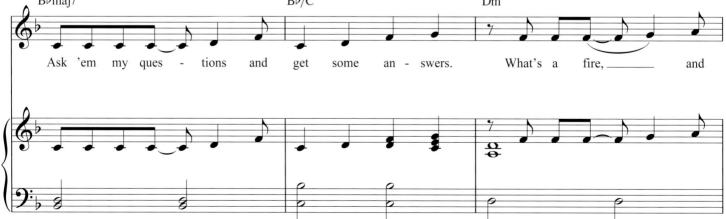

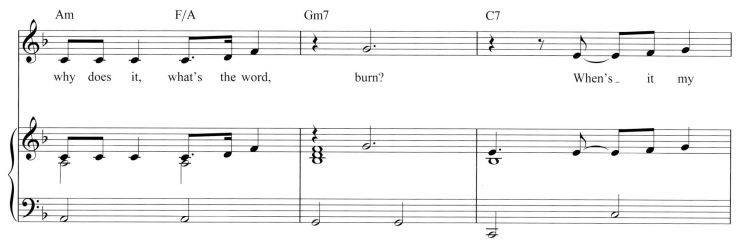

why does it, what's the word, burn? When's it my

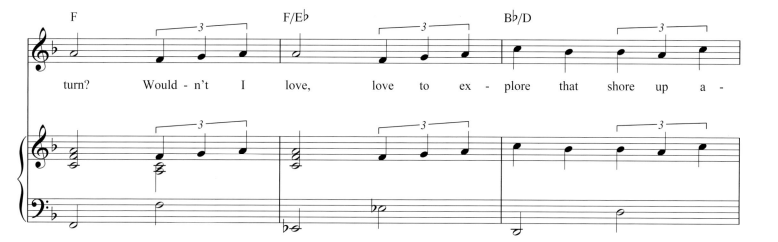

turn? Would-n't I love, love to ex - plore that shore up a -

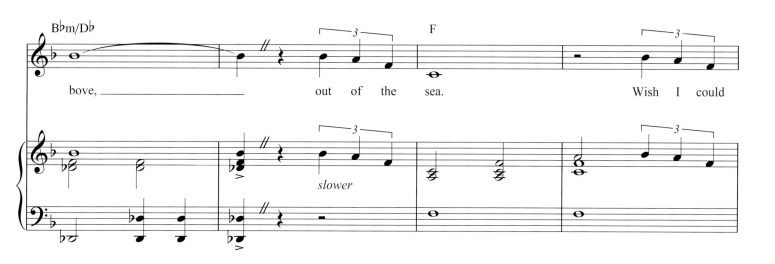

bove, out of the sea. Wish I could

be part of that world.

Under the Sea
From *THE LITTLE MERMAID*

Music by ALAN MENKEN
Lyrics by HOWARD ASHMAN

Brightly

The sea - weed is al - ways green - er in some - bod - y
Down here ___ all the fish is hap - py as off ___ through the

else - 's lake. You dream ___ a - bout go - ing up there.
waves dey roll. The fish ___ on the land ain't hap - py.

But that ___ is a big mis - take. Just look ___ at the
They sad ___ 'cause they in the bowl. But fish ___ in the

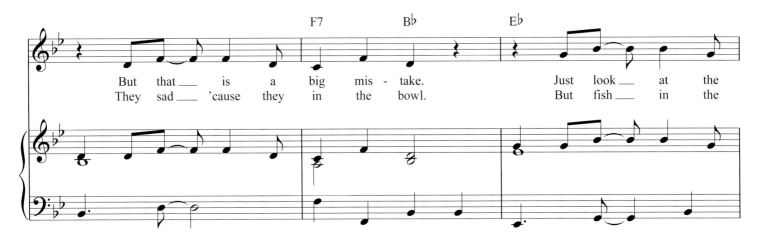

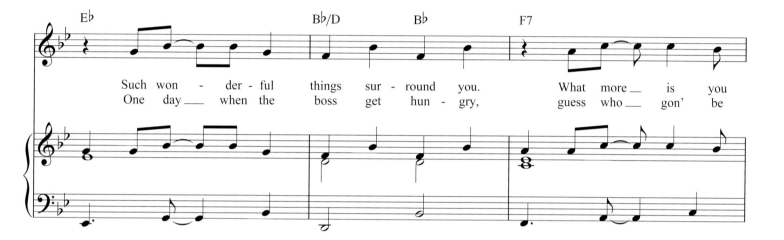

wet-ter. Take _ it from me.
eat us in _ fri - ca - see.
Up _ on the shore they work _ all day.
We _ what the land folks loves _ to cook.

Out _ in the sun they slave _ a - way.
Un - der the sea we off _ the hook.
While _ we de -
We _ got no

vot - in' full - time to float - in' un - der the sea.
trou - bles, life _ is the bub - bles un - der the

sea.

Under the Sea

From *THE LITTLE MERMAID*

Music by Alan Menken
Lyrics by Howard Ashman

The seaweed is always greener in somebody else's lake
You dream about going up there
But that is a big mistake
Just look at the world around you, right here on the ocean floor
Such wonderful things surround you
What more is you lookin' for?
Under the sea, under the sea
Darlin' it's better down where it's wetter
Take it from me
Up on the shore they work all day
Out in the sun they slave away
While we devotin' full time to floatin' under the sea
Down here all the fish is happy as off through the waves they roll
The fish on the land ain't happy
They sad 'cause they in the bowl
But fish in the bowl is lucky, they in for a worser fate
One day when the boss get hungry guess who's gon' be on the plate?
Under the sea, under the sea
Nobody beat us, fry us and eat us in fricassee
We what the land folks loves to cook
Under the sea we off the hook
We got no troubles life is the bubbles under the sea
Under the sea
Since life is sweet here we got the beat here naturally
Even the sturgeon an' the ray they get the urge 'n' start to play
We got the spirit, you got to hear it under the sea
The newt can play the flute
The carp play the harp
The plaice play the bass
And they soundin' sharp
The bass play the brass
The chub play the tub
The fluke is the duke of soul
The ray he can play
The lings on the strings
The trout rockin' out
The blackfish she sings
The smelt and the sprat they know where it's at
An' oh, that blowfish blow
Under the sea
Under the sea
When the sardine begin the beguine it's music to me
What do they got, a lot of sand
We got a hot crustacean band
Each little clam here know how to jam here under the sea
Each little slug here cuttin' a rug here under the sea
Each little snail here know how to wail here
That's why it's hotter under the water
Ya we in luck here down in the muck here under the sea

Be Our Guest

From *BEAUTY AND THE BEAST*

Music by ALAN MENKEN
Lyrics by HOWARD ASHMAN

Be our guest! Be our guest! Put our ser-vice to the

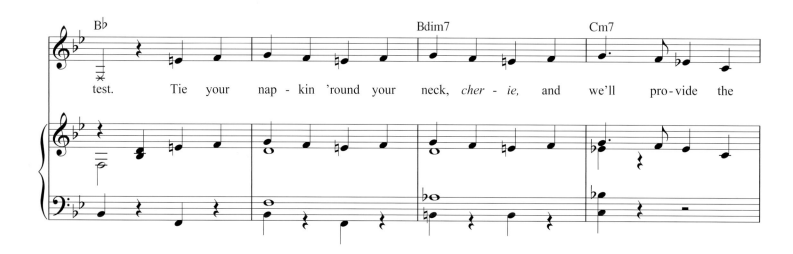

test. Tie your nap-kin 'round your neck, *cher-ie,* and we'll pro-vide the

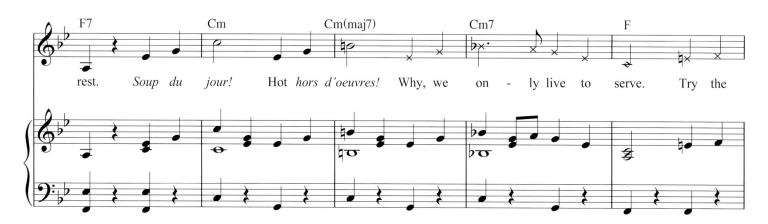

rest. *Soup du jour!* Hot *hors d'oeuvres!* Why, we on-ly live to serve. Try the

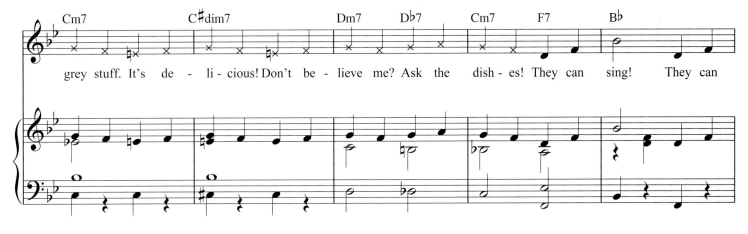

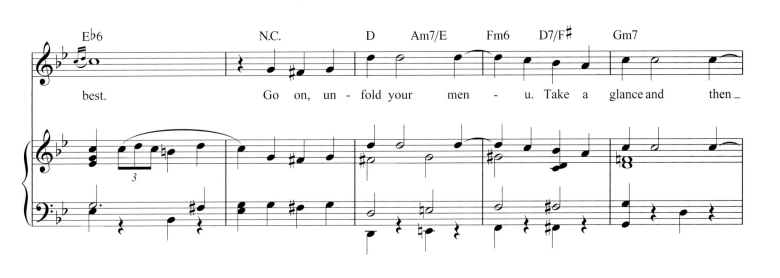

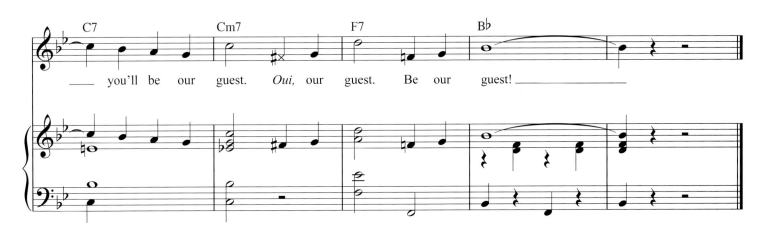

Be Our Guest

From *BEAUTY AND THE BEAST*

Music by Alan Menken
Lyrics by Howard Ashman

Lumiere: *Ma chere Mademoiselle,*
It is with deepest pride and greatest pleasure that we welcome you tonight.
And now, we invite you to relax.
Let us pull up a chair as the dining room proudly presents your dinner!

Be our guest!
Be our guest!
Put our service to the test
Tie your napkin 'round your neck, cherie
And we provide the rest

Soup du jour!
Hot hors d'oeuvres!
Why, we only live to serve
Try the grey stuff, it's delicious!
Don't believe me?
Ask the dishes!

They can sing!
They can dance!
After all, Miss, this is France!
And a dinner here is never second best

Go on, unfold your menu
Take a glance
And then you'll be our guest
Oui, our guest!
Be our guest!

Beef ragout!
Cheese souffle!
Pie and pudding "en flambe!"
We'll prepare and serve with flair
A culinary cabaret!

You're alone and you're scared
But the banquet's all prepared
No one's gloomy or complaining
While the flatware's entertaining

We tell jokes
I do tricks with my fellow candlesticks

Mugs: And it's all in perfect taste
That you can bet!

All: Come on and lift your glass
You've won your own free pass
To be our guest!

Lumiere: If you're stressed
It's fine dining we suggest

All: Be our guest!
Be our guest!
Be our guest!

Lumiere: Life is so unnerving for a servant who's not serving
He's not whole without a soul to wait upon
Ah those good old days when we were useful
Suddenly, those good old days are gone

Ten years, we've been rusting
Needing so much more – than dusting
Needing exercise, a chance to use our skills

Most days, we just lay around the castle
Flabby, fat and lazy
You walked in and oops-a-daisy

Mrs. Potts: It's a guest!
It's a guest!
Sakes alive
We'll I'll be blessed!
Wine's been poured and thank the Lord
I've had the napkins freshly pressed

With dessert she'll want tea
And my dear, that's fine with me
While the cups do their soft shoeing
I'll be bubbling!
I'll be brewing!

I'll get warm, piping hot!
Heaven's sakes!
Is that a spot?
Clean it up!
We want the company impressed!

We've got a lot to do
Is it one lump or two
For you, our guest?

Chorus: She's our guest!

Mrs. Potts: She's our guest!

Chorus: She's our guest!
Be our guest!
Be our guest!

Our command is your request
It's been years since we had anybody here
And we're obsessed

With your meal
With your ease
Yes, indeed
We aim to please

While the candlelight's still glowing
Let us help you
We'll keep going

Course by course
One by one!
Till you shout
"Enough. I'm done!"
Then we'll sing you off to sleep as you digest

Tonight you'll prop your feet up!
But for now, let's eat up!

Be our guest!
Be our guest!
Be our guest!
Please, be our guest!

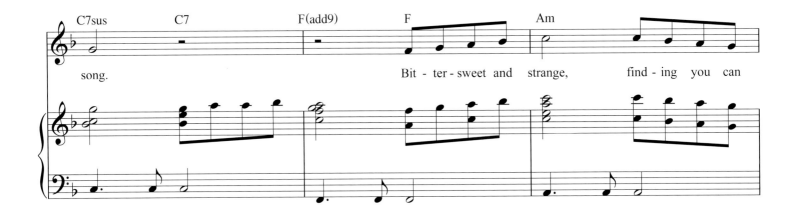

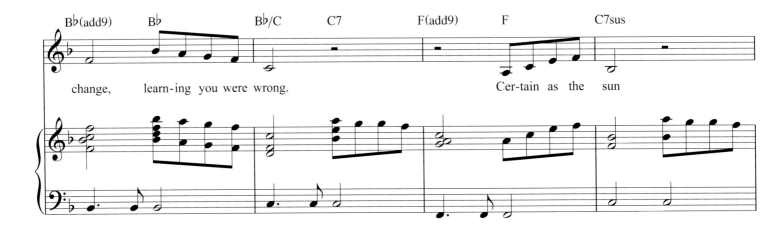

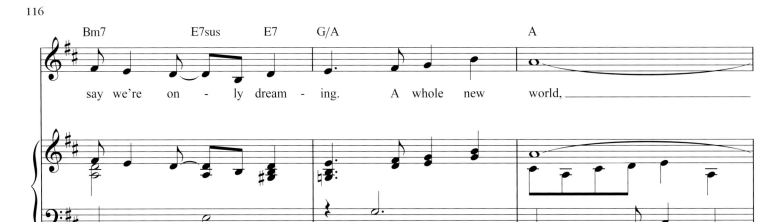

say we're on - ly dream - ing. A whole new world,

a daz - zling place I nev - er knew. But when I'm

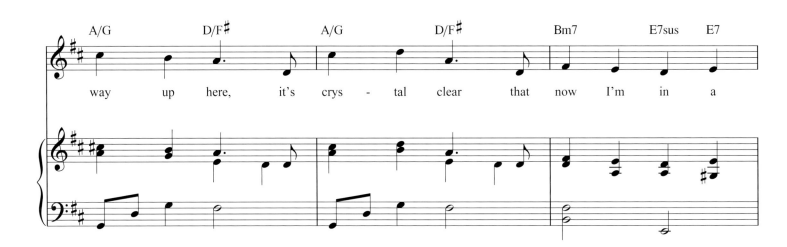

way up here, it's crys - tal clear that now I'm in a

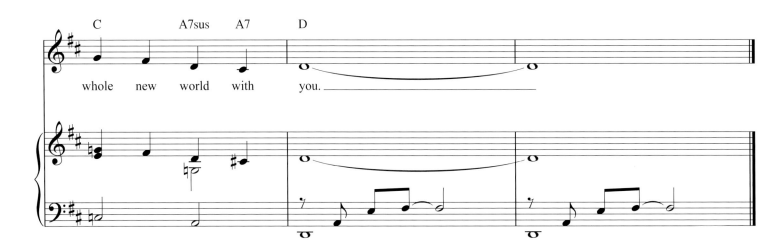

whole new world with you.

A Whole New World

From *ALADDIN*

Music by Alan Menken
Lyrics by Tim Rice

Aladdin:	I can show you the world
	Shining, shimmering, splendid
	Tell me princess, now
	When did you last let your heart decide?
	I can open your eyes
	Take you wonder by wonder
	Over, sideways and under on a magic carpet ride
	A whole new world
	A new fantastic point of view
	No one to tell us no or where to go
	Or say we're only dreaming
Jasmine:	A whole new world
	A dazzling place I never knew
	But when I'm way up here it's crystal clear
	That now I'm in a whole new world with you
Aladdin:	Now I'm in a whole new world with you
Jasmine:	Unbelievable sights, indescribable feeling
	Soaring, tumbling, free-wheeling
	Through an endless diamond sky
	A whole new world
Aladdin:	Don't you dare close your eyes
Jasmine:	A hundred thousand things to see
Aladdin:	Hold your breath, it gets better
Jasmine:	I'm like a shooting star I've come so far
	I can't go back to where I used to be
Aladdin:	A whole new world
Jasmine:	Ev'ry turn a surprise
Aladdin:	With new horizons to pursue
Jasmine:	Ev'ry moment red-letter
Both:	I'll chase them anywhere. There's time to spare
	Let me share this whole new world with you
Aladdin:	A whole new world
Jasmine:	A whole new world
Aladdin:	That's where we'll be
Jasmine:	That's where we'll be
Aladdin:	A thrilling chase
Jasmine:	A wondrous place
Both:	For you and me

Friend Like Me

From *ALADDIN*

Music by ALAN MENKEN
Lyrics by HOWARD ASHMAN

Bright Two-beat

Well, A-li Ba-ba had them for-ty thieves. She-he-ra-za-de had a thou-sand tales.

But, mas-ter, you in luck 'cause up your sleeves you got a

brand of mag-ic nev-er fails. You got some pow-er in your

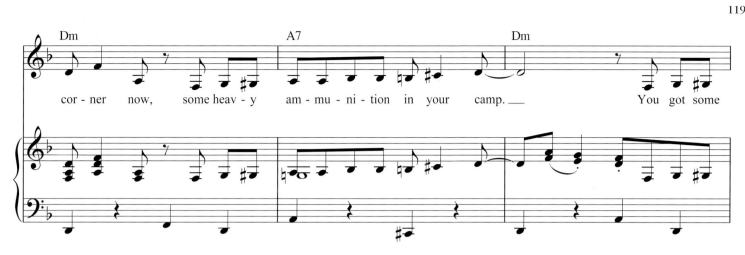

cor - ner now, some heav - y am - mu - ni - tion in your camp. ___ You got some

punch, pi - zazz, ya - hoo, and how! ___ See, all you got - ta do is rub that lamp.

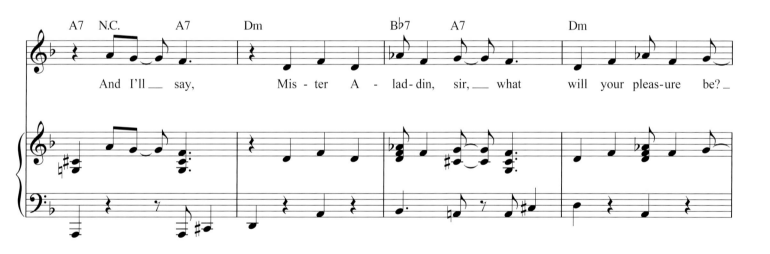

And I'll ___ say, Mis - ter A - lad - din, sir, ___ what will your pleas - ure be? ___

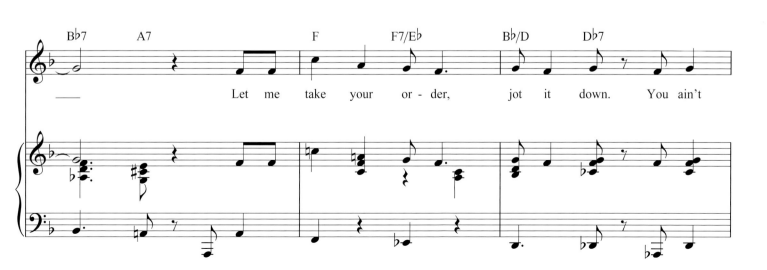

___ Let me take your or - der, jot it down. You ain't

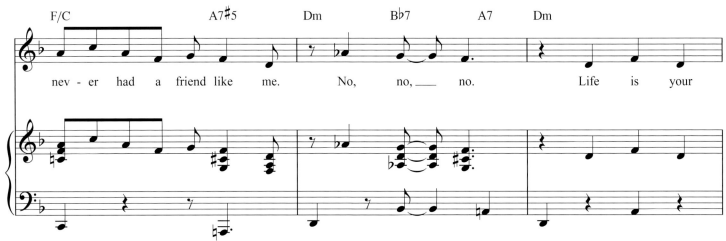

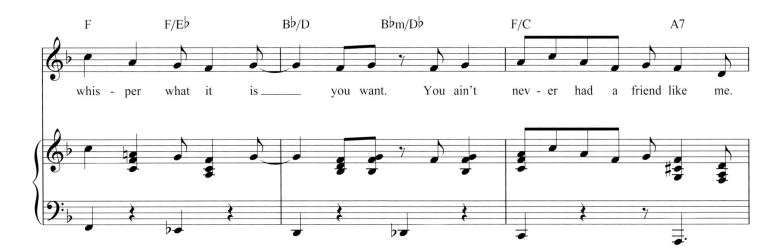

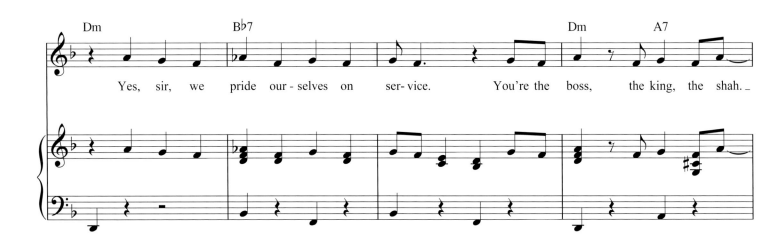

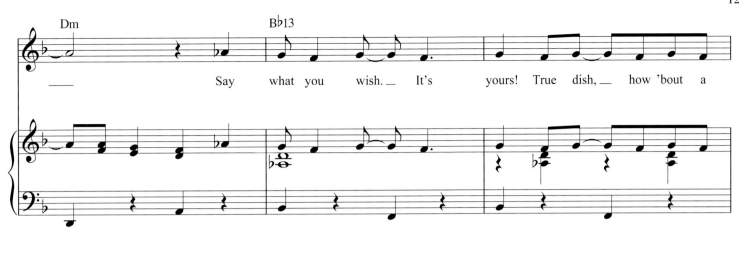

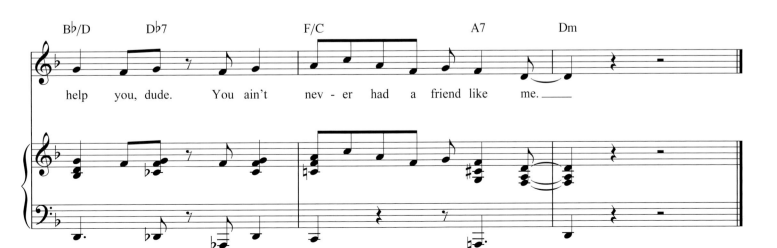

Friend Like Me

From *ALADDIN*

Music by Alan Menken
Lyrics by Howard Ashman

We'll, Ali Baba had them forty thieves
Scheherazade had a thousand tales
But, master, you in luck 'cause up your sleeves
You got a brand of magic never fails
You got some power in your corner now
Some heavy ammunition in your camp
You got some punch, pizazz, yahoo and how
See, all you gotta do is rub that lamp
And I'll say, Mister Aladdin, sir
What will your pleasure be?
Let me take your order, jot it down
You ain't never had a friend like me. No no no
Life is your restaurant and I'm your maitre d'
C'mon whisper what it is you want
You ain't never had a friend like me
Yes sir, we pride ourselves on service
You're the boss, the king, the shah
Say what you wish. It's yours!
True dish, how 'bout a little more baklava?
Have some of column "A"
Try all of column "B"
I'm in the mood to help you, dude
You ain't never had a friend like me
Wa-ah-ah. Oh my
Wa-ah-ah. No, no
Wa-ah-ah. Na nan a
Can your friends do this?
Can your friends do that?
Can your friends pull this out their little hat?
Can your friends go poof?
Well looky here.
Can your friends go abracadabra
Let 'er rip and then make the sucker disappear?
So doncha sit there slack-jawed, buggy-eyed
I'm here to answer all your midday prayers
You got me bona fide certified
You got a genie for your chargé d'affaires
I got a powerful urge to help you out
So whatcha wish I really want to know
You got a list that's three miles long, no doubt
Well, all you gotta do is rub like so. And oh
Mister Aladdin, sir, have a wish or two or three
I'm on the job, you big nabob
You ain't never had a friend, never had a friend
You ain't never had a friend, never had a friend
You ain't never had a friend like me
Wa-ah-ah. Wa-ah-ah
You ain't never had a friend like me. Ha!

Circle of Life

From *THE LION KING*

Music by ELTON JOHN
Lyrics by TIM RICE

Relaxed Pop beat

From the day we ar-rive on the plan - et and
Some of us fall by the way - side, and

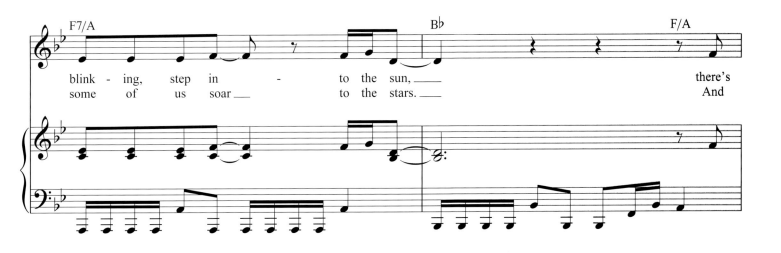

blink - ing, step in - to the sun, there's
some of us soar to the stars. And

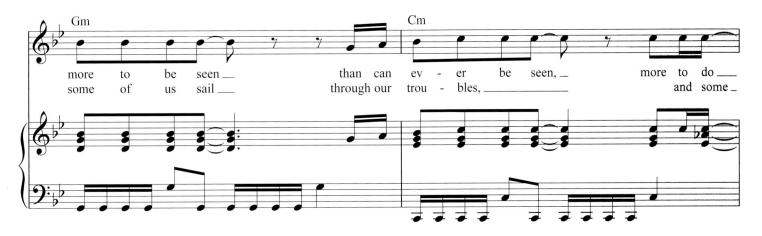

more to be seen than can ev - er be seen, more to do
some of us sail through our trou - bles, and some

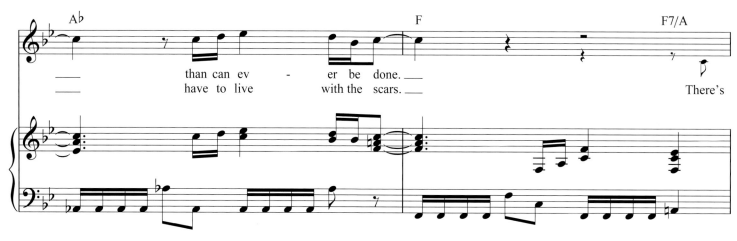

than can ev - er be done. ___
have to live with the scars. ___
There's

Some say, "Eat or be eat - en." ___ Some say, ___
far too much ___ to take in here, more to

___ find "Live and let live." ___ But
than can ev - er be found. ___ But the

all are a - greed ___ as they join the stam - pede, ___ you should
sun roll - ing high ___ through the sap - phi - re sky ___ keeps great and

cresc.

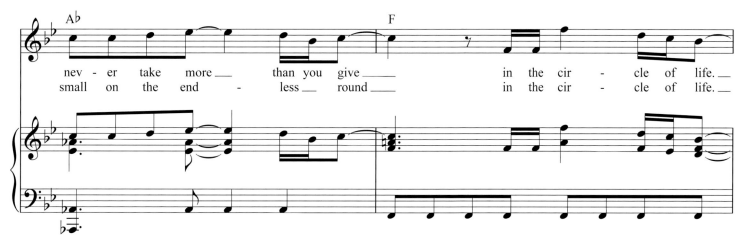

never take more ___ than you give ___ in the cir - cle of life. ___
small on the end - less ___ round ___ in the cir - cle of life. ___

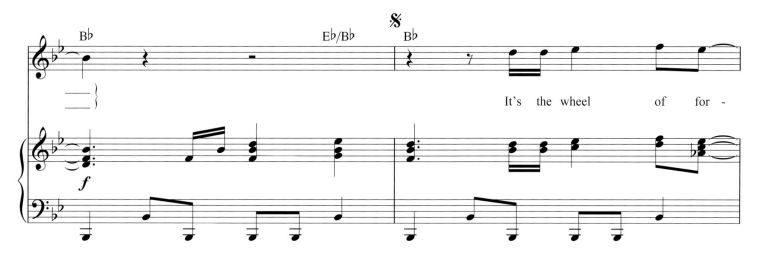

It's the wheel of for -

- tune. It's the leap of faith. ___

It's the band of ___ hope ___

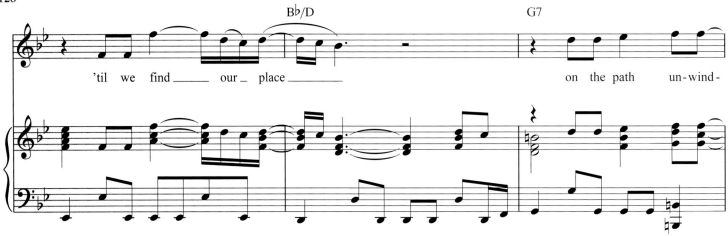

'til we find _____ our _ place _____ on the path un-wind-

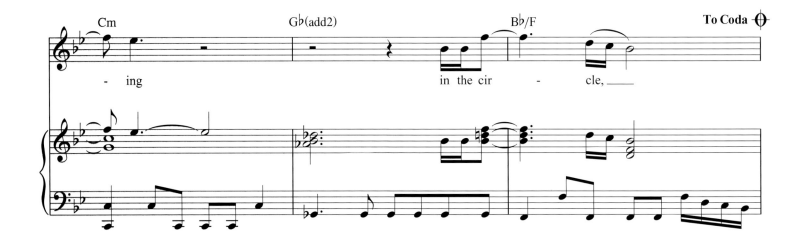

- ing in the cir - cle, _____

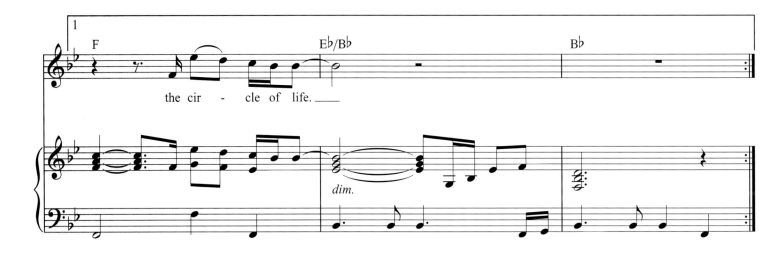

the cir - cle of life. _____

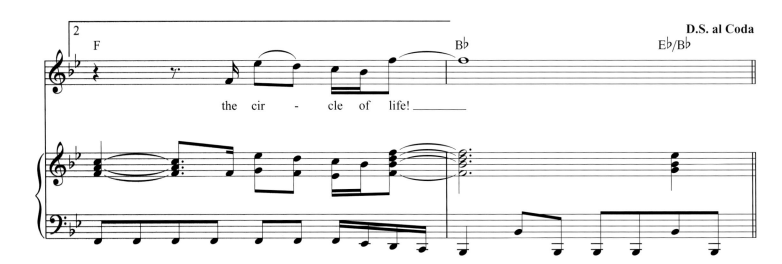

the cir - cle of life! _____

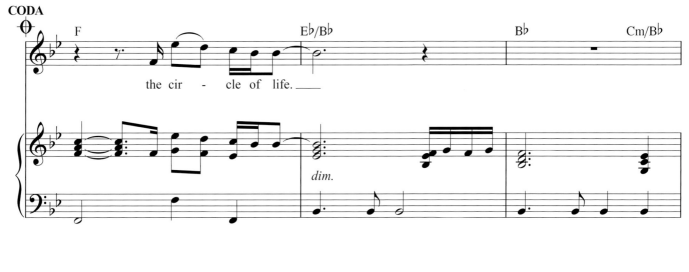

the cir - cle of life. ____

On the path un - wind - ing

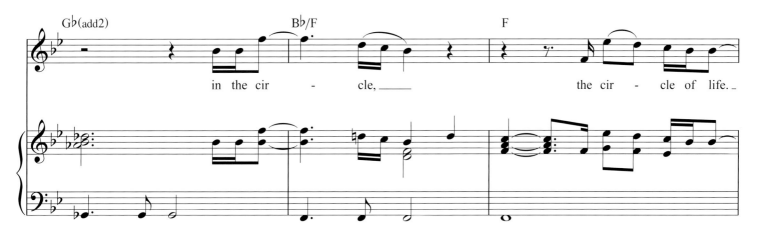

in the cir - cle, ____ the cir - cle of life. _

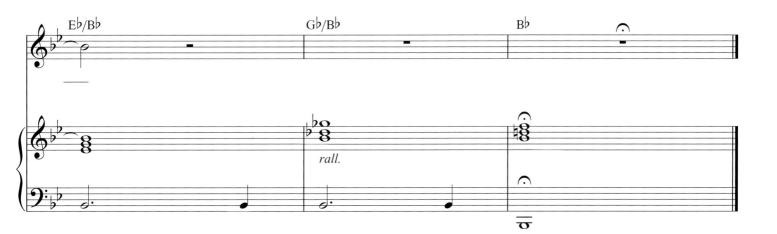

Can You Feel the Love Tonight

From *THE LION KING*

Music by ELTON JOHN
Lyrics by TIM RICE

Pop Ballad

There's a calm sur-ren-der to the rush of day,
There's a time for ev-'ry-one, if they on-ly learn

when the heat of the roll-ing world can be turned a-way.
that the twist-ing ka-lei-do-scope moves us all in turn.

An en-chant-ed mo-ment, and it sees me through.
There's a rhyme and rea-son to the wild out-doors

It's e - nough_ for this rest - less war - rior just to be __ with you. __
when the heart __ of this star-crossed voy-ag - er beats in time __ with yours. __
And

can you feel __ the love ____ to - night? _____

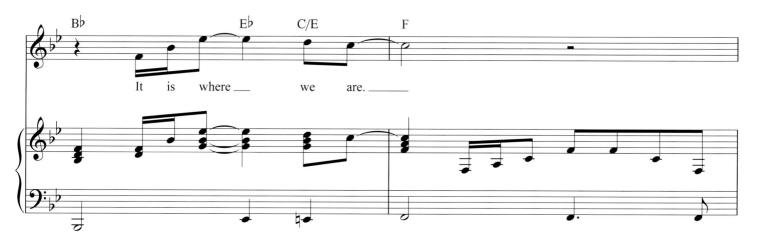

It is where __ we are. _____

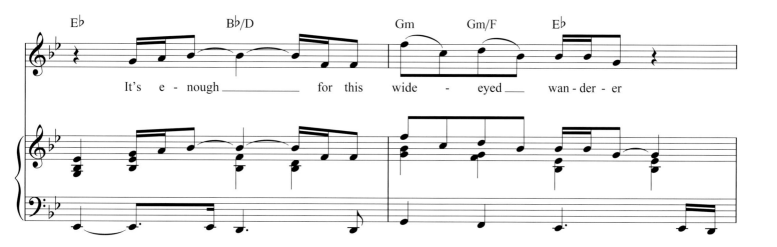

It's e - nough _____ for this wide - eyed __ wan - der - er

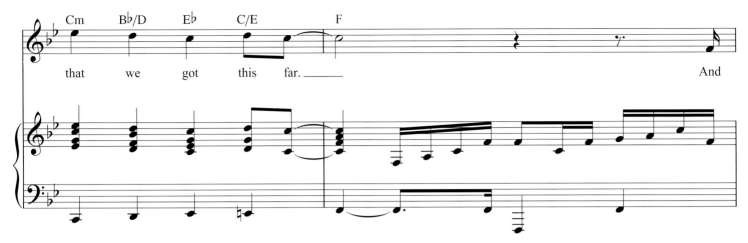

that we got this far.____ And

can you feel ___ the love ___ to - night, _____

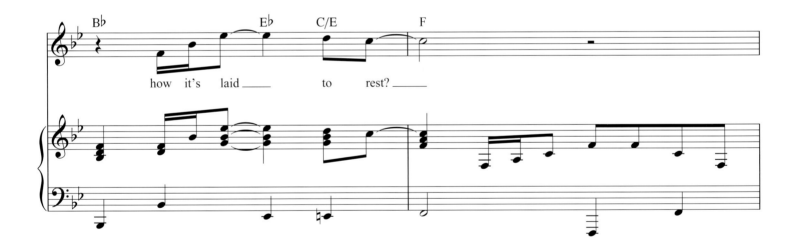

how it's laid ___ to rest? _____

It's e - nough _____ to make kings ___ and ___ vag - a - bonds ___ be -

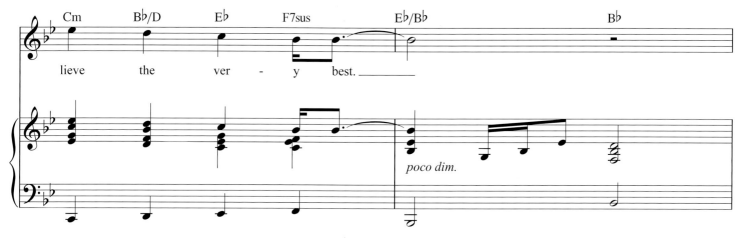

lieve the ver - y best. _____

It's e - nough _____ to make kings _ and _ vag-a-bonds _ be-

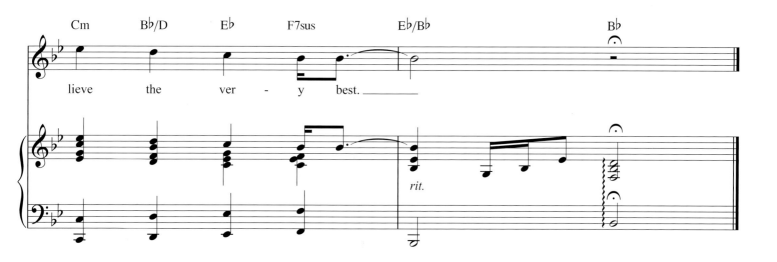

lieve the ver - y best. _____

Hakuna Matata

From *THE LION KING*

Music by ELTON JOHN
Lyrics by TIM RICE

for the rest of your days. _____ It's our

prob-lem - free _____ phi - los - o - phy. __

Ha - ku - na ma - ta - ta. _____ *Simba: Hakuna matata?*

Pumbaa: Yeah. It's our motto.   *Simba: What's a motto?*   *Timon: Nothin'! What's - a - motto with you?!*

Slower

Pumbaa: *Those two words will solve all your problems.*   Timon: *That's right. Take Pumbaa here.*   Why... when

Timon:

he was a young wart - hog... When I was a young wart - hog! *Timon: Very nice.* He
Pumbaa: Thanks.

In tempo, brightly

found his a - ro - ma lacked a cer - tain ap - peal. __ He could clear the Sa - van - nah af - ter

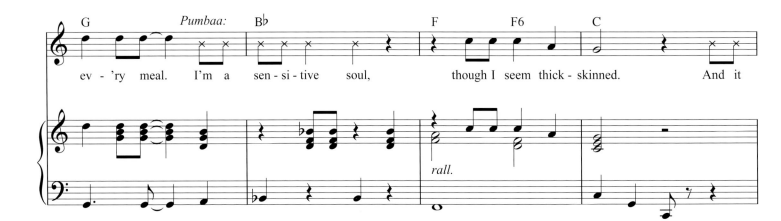

ev - 'ry meal. I'm a sen - si - tive soul, though I seem thick - skinned. And it

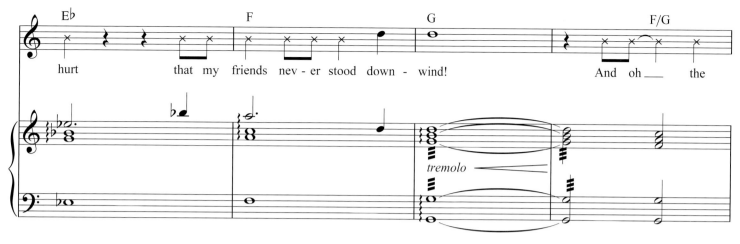

hurt that my friends nev-er stood down-wind! And oh ___ the

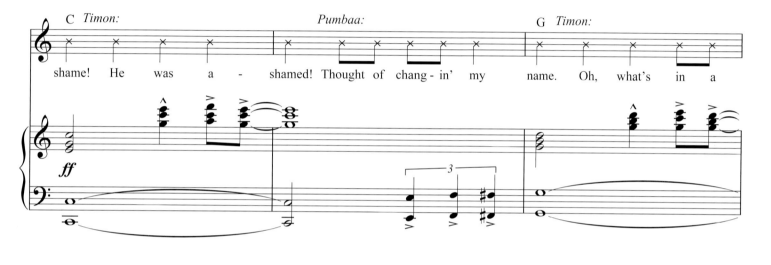

shame! He was a-shamed! Thought of chang-in' my name. Oh, what's in a

name? And I got down-heart-ed. How did ya feel? ___ Ev-'ry time that I...

In tempo

Timon: Hey, Pumbaa.
Not in front of the kids!
Pumbaa: Oh, sorry.

Ha-ku - na ma-ta-ta! What a won-der-ful

phrase. Ha-ku-na ma-ta-ta ain't no pass-ing

craze! *Young Simba:* It means no wor-ries for the rest___ of your days.___

Young Simba, Timon & Pumbaa: It's our prob-lem-free___ phi-

Timon & Young Simba: los-o-phy.___ Ha-ku-na ma-ta-ta.___

Hakuna Matata

From *THE LION KING*

Music by Elton John
Lyrics by Tim Rice

Timon:	*Hakuna matata…what a wonderful phrase!*
Pumbaa:	*Hakuna matata…ain't no passing craze*
Timon:	It means no worries for the rest of your days
Timon & Pumbaa:	It's our problem-free philosophy
Timon:	Hakuna matata
Simba:	*Hakuna matata?*
Pumbaa:	*Yeah, it's our motto.*
Simba:	*What's a motto?*
Timon:	*Nothin'! What's-a-motto with you?!*
Pumbaa:	*Those two words will solve all your problems.*
Timon:	*That's right. Take Pumbaa here.*
	Why, when he was a young warthog…
Pumbaa:	When I was a young warthog!
Timon:	*Very nice.*
Pumbaa:	*Thanks.*
Timon:	He found his aroma lacked a certain appeal
	He could clear the savannah after ev'ry meal!
Pumbaa:	I'm a sensitive soul, though I seem thick-skinned
	And it hurt that my friends never stood downwind!
	And, oh, the shame!
Timon:	He was ashamed!
Pumbaa:	Thought of changin' my name!
Timon:	Oh, what's in a name?
Pumbaa:	And I got downhearted…
Timon:	How did you feel?
Pumbaa:	…ev'ry time that I…
Timon:	*Hey, Pumbaa, not in front of the kids.*
Pumbaa:	*Oh, sorry.*
Timon & Pumbaa:	Hakuna matata…what a wonderful phrase
	Hakuna matata…ain't no passing craze
Simba:	It means no worries for the rest of your days
Timon:	*Yeah, sing it kid!*
Timon & Simba:	It's our problem-free
Pumbaa:	Philosophy
All:	Hakuna matata
	Hakuna matata. Hakuna matata
	Hakuna matata. Hakuna…
Timon:	It means no worries for the rest of your days
All:	It's our problem-free philosophy
Timon:	Hakuna matata
Pumba:	Hakuna matata. Hakuna matata
Timon:	Hakuna matata
Pumba:	Hakuna matata
Timon:	Hakuna matata. Hakuna matata
	Hakuna matata. Hakuna matata

Colors of the Wind

From *POCAHONTAS*

Music by ALAN MENKEN
Lyrics by STEPHEN SCHWARTZ

Moderately

You think you own _ what-ev-er land _ you land on;
think the on - ly peo-ple who _ are peo - ple

the
are the

earth is just a dead thing you can claim;
peo - ple _ who look and think like you.

but

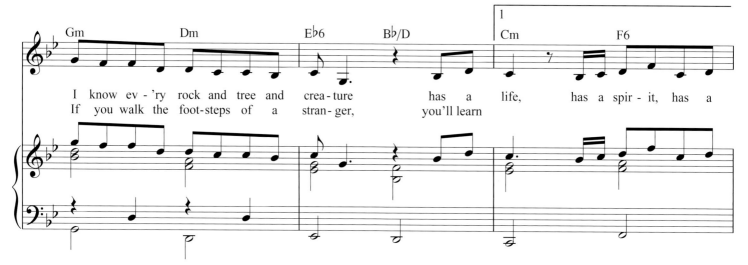

I know ev - 'ry rock and tree and crea - ture has a life, has a spir - it, has a
If you walk the foot-steps of a stran - ger, you'll learn

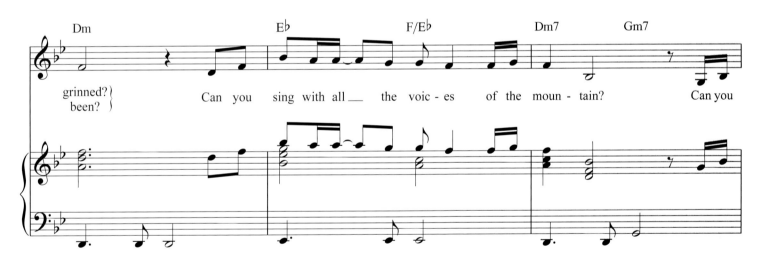

wind?　　Come run the hid-den pine＿trails of the
rain-storm and the riv － er are my

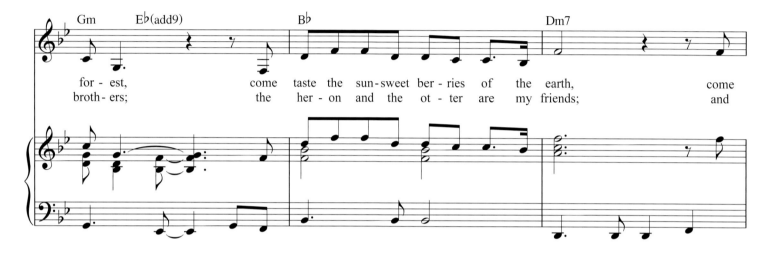

for - est,　　come taste the sun-sweet ber - ries of the earth,　　come
broth - ers;　　the her - on and the ot - ter are my friends;　　and

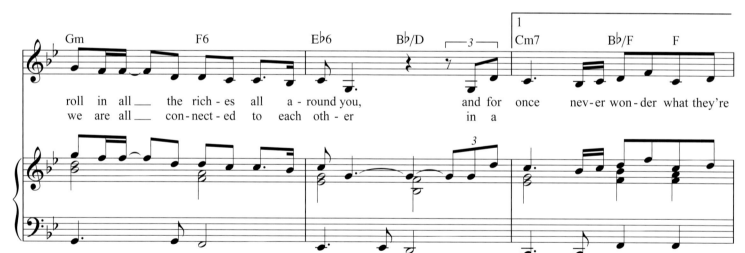

roll in all＿ the rich - es all a - round you,　　and for once nev-er won-der what they're
we are all＿ con-nect - ed to each oth - er　　　in a

D.S. al Coda

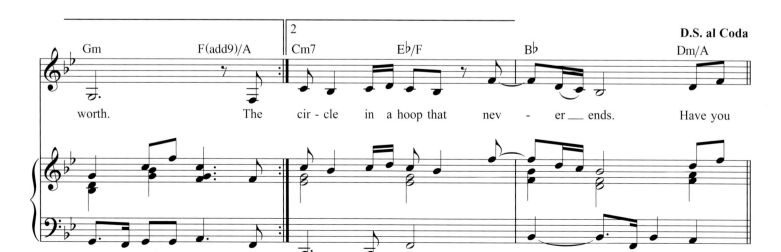

worth.　　The cir - cle in a hoop that nev - er＿ends.　　Have you

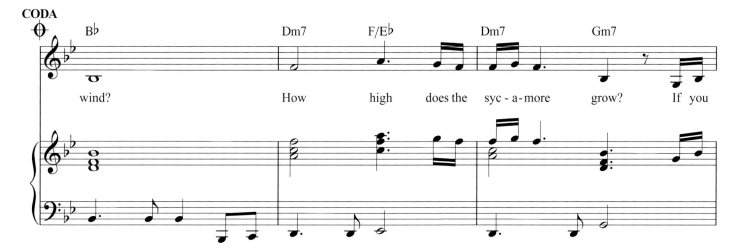

CODA

Bb — Dm7 — F/Eb — Dm7 — Gm7

wind? How high does the syc-a-more grow? If you

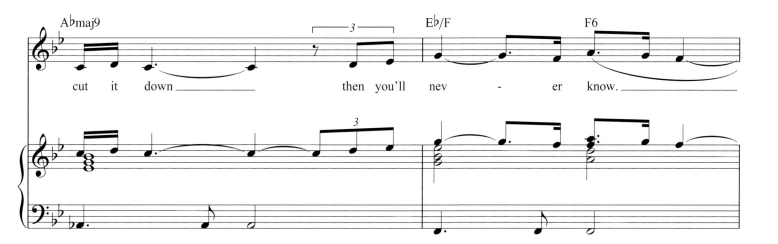

Abmaj9 — Eb/F — F6

cut it down _____ then you'll nev - er know. _____

Eb/F — F — Gm — Dm7 — Eb — F

_____ And you'll nev - er hear the wolf cry to the blue corn moon, for

rall. *a tempo*

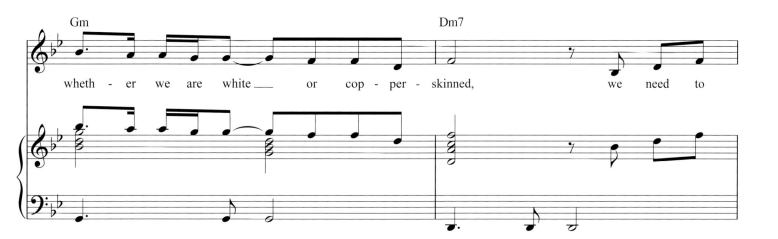

Gm — Dm7

wheth - er we are white ___ or cop - per - skinned, we need to

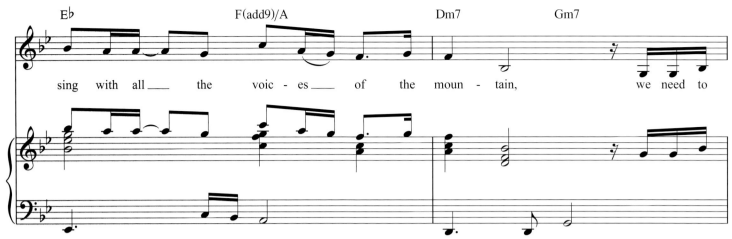

sing with all ___ the voic - es ___ of the moun - tain, we need to

paint with all ___ the col-ors of the wind. You can own the earth ___ and still all you'll

own is earth un - til you can paint with all the col - ors of the wind.

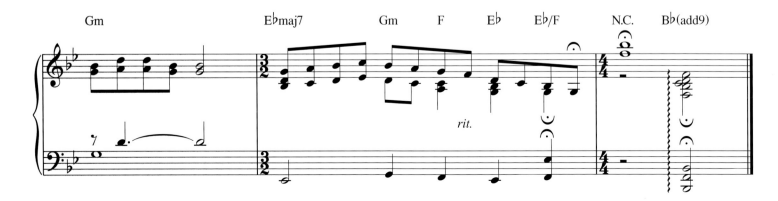

Colors of the Wind
From *POCAHONTAS*

Music by Alan Menken
Lyrics by Stephen Schwartz

You think you own whatever land you land on
The earth is just a dead thing you can claim
But I know ev'ry rock and tree and creature
Has a life, has a spirit, has a name
You think the only people who are people
Are the people who look and think like you
But if you walk the footsteps of a stranger
You'll learn things you never knew you never knew
Have you ever heard the wolf cry to the blue corn moon
Or asked the grinning bobcat why he grinned?
Can you sing with all the voices of the mountain?
Can you paint with all the colors of the wind?
Can you paint with all the colors of the wind?
Come run the hidden pine trails of the forest
Come taste the sun-sweet berries of the earth
Come roll in all the riches all around you
And for once never wonder what they're worth
The rainstorm and the river are my brothers
The heron and the otter are my friends
And we are all connected to each other
In a circle in a hoop that never ends
Have you ever heard the wolf cry to the blue corn moon
Or let the eagle tell you where he's been?
Can you sing with all the voices of the mountain?
Can you paint with all the colors of the wind?
Can you paint with all the colors of the wind?
How high does the sycamore grow?
If you cut it down then you'll never know
And you'll never hear the wolf cry to the blue corn moon
For whether we are white or copper-skinned
We need to sing with all the voices of the mountain
We need to paint with all the colors of the wind
You can own the earth and still all you'll own is earth until
You can paint with all the colors of the wind

You've Got a Friend in Me

From *TOY STORY*

Music and Lyrics by
RANDY NEWMAN

Easy Shuffle

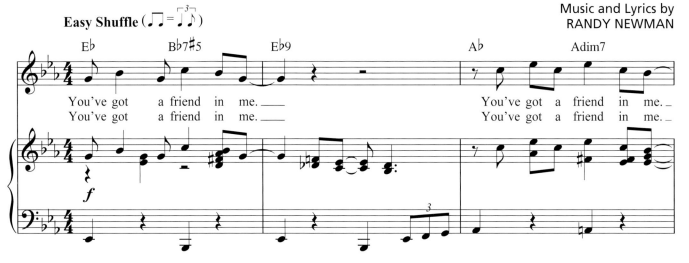

You've got a friend in me. ___ You've got a friend in me. _
You've got a friend in me. ___ You've got a friend in me. _

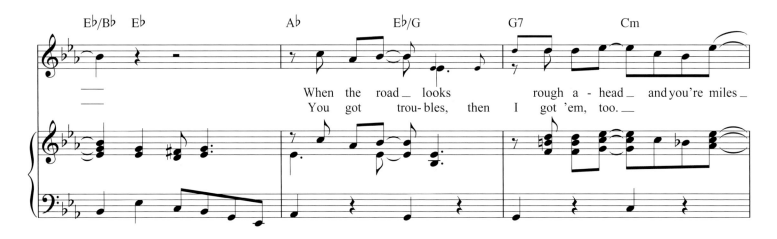

___ When the road ___ looks rough a - head ___ and you're miles ___
You got trou - bles, then I got 'em, too. _

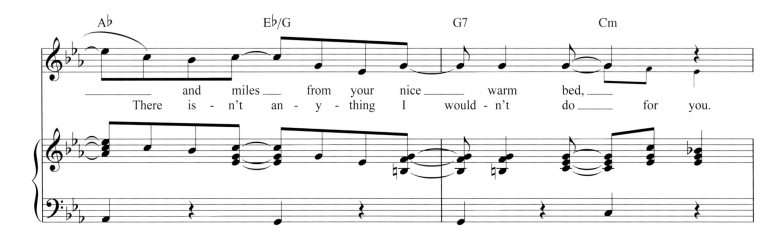

___ and miles ___ from your nice ___ warm bed, ___
There is - n't an - y - thing I would - n't do ___ for you.

you just re-mem-ber what your old pal said:____ Son, you've____
If we stick to-geth-er we can see it through,___ 'cause you've____

____ got a friend in me.____ Yeah, you've____ got a friend in me.
____ got a friend in me.____ Yeah, you've____ got a friend in me.

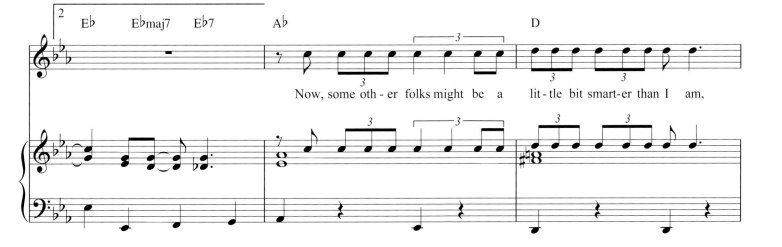

Now, some oth-er folks might be a lit-tle bit smart-er than I am,

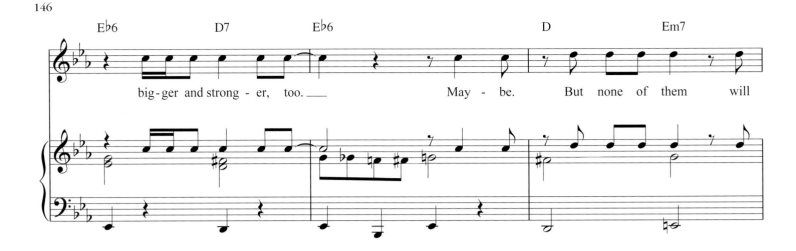

big-ger and strong-er, too. ___ May - be. But none of them will

ev - er love ___ you the way ___ I do, ___ just me and you, ___ boy.

And as the years go by, ___ our friend-ship will nev - er die. __

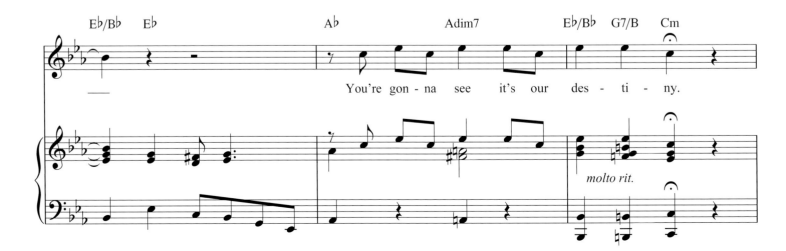

You're gon - na see it's our des - ti - ny.

molto rit.

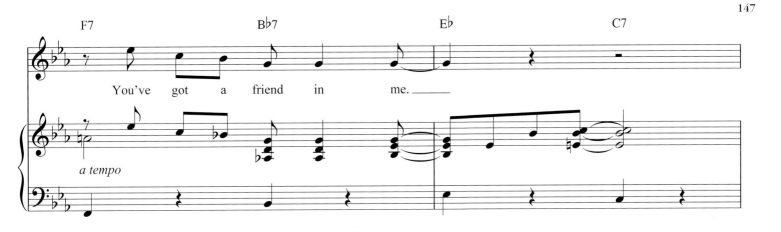

You've got a friend in me. _____

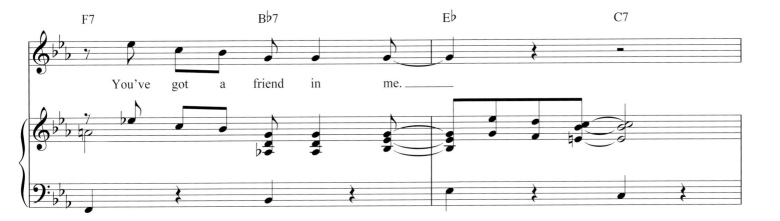

You've got a friend in me. _____

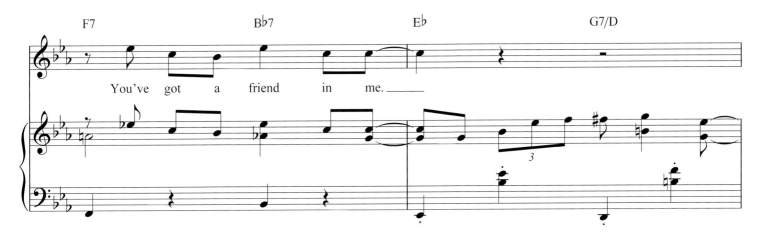

You've got a friend in me. _____

God Help the Outcasts

From *THE HUNCHBACK OF NOTRE DAME*

Music by ALAN MENKEN
Lyrics by STEPHEN SCHWARTZ

God help the out-casts, hun-gry from birth.
I ask for noth-ing, I can get by. But

Show them the mer-cy they don't find on earth.
I know so man-y less luck-y than I. The

lost and for-got-ten, they look to You still.
God help the out-casts, the poor and down-trod.

149

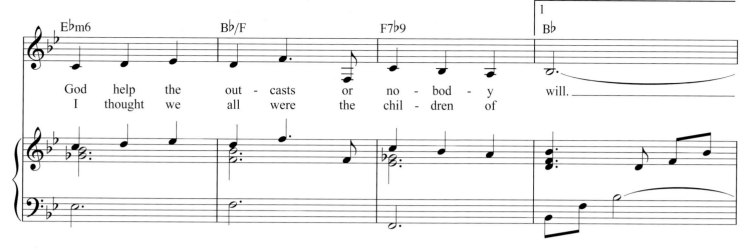

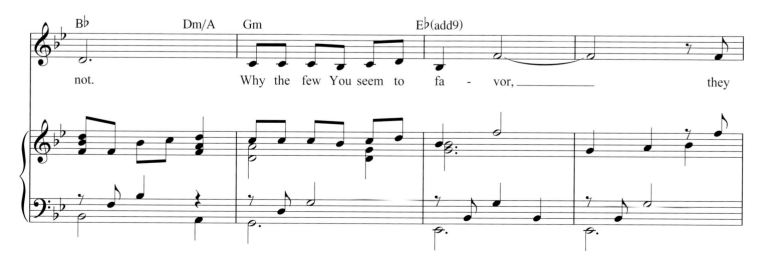

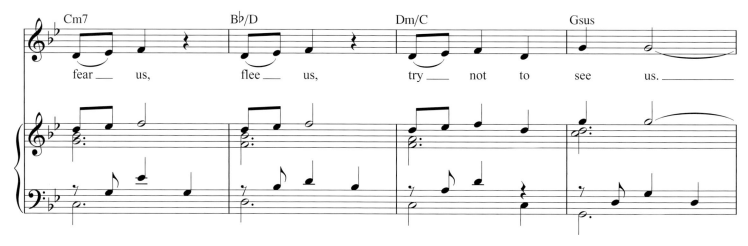

fear ___ us,   flee ___ us,   try ___ not to   see   us. ___

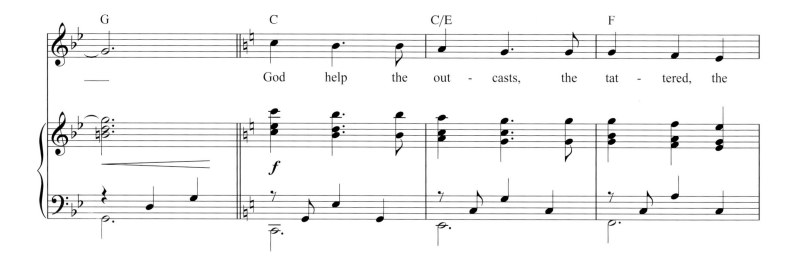

God help the out - casts, the tat - tered, the

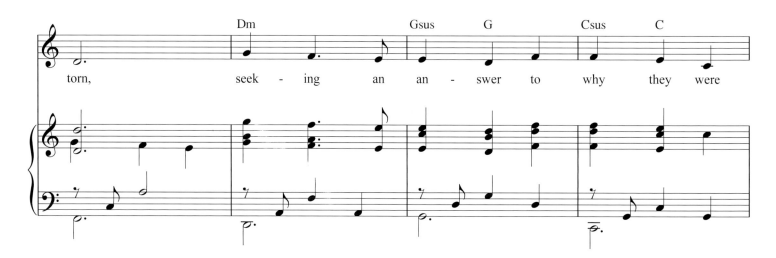

torn,   seek - ing an an - swer to why they were

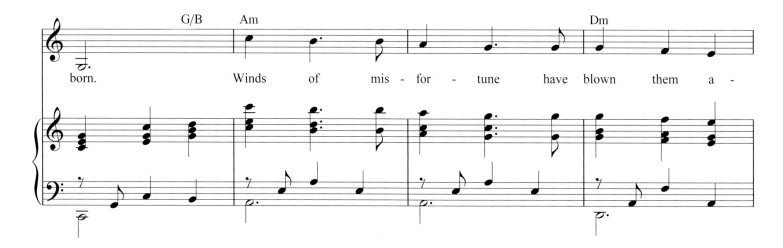

born.   Winds of mis - for - tune have blown them a -

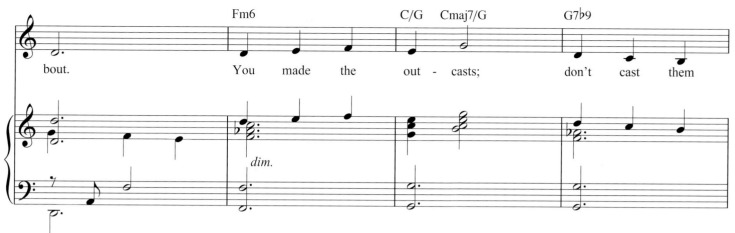

bout. You made the out - casts; don't cast them

out. The poor and un - luck - y, the

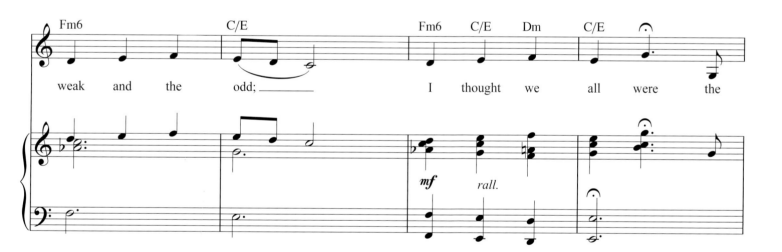

weak and the odd; _____ I thought we all were the

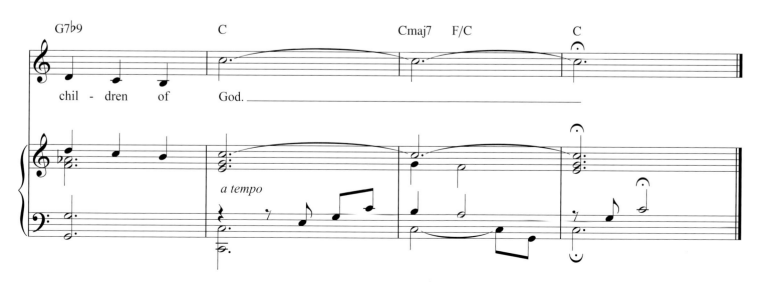

chil - dren of God. _____

Someday

From *THE HUNCHBACK OF NOTRE DAME*

Music by ALAN MENKEN
Lyrics by STEPHEN SCHWARTZ

Tenderly

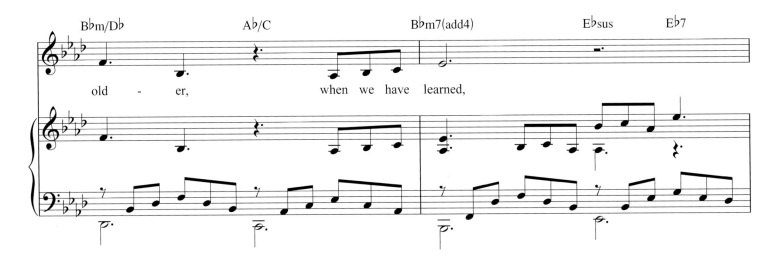

Some-day when we are wis - er, when the world's

old - er, when we have learned,

I pray some-day we may yet live to

153

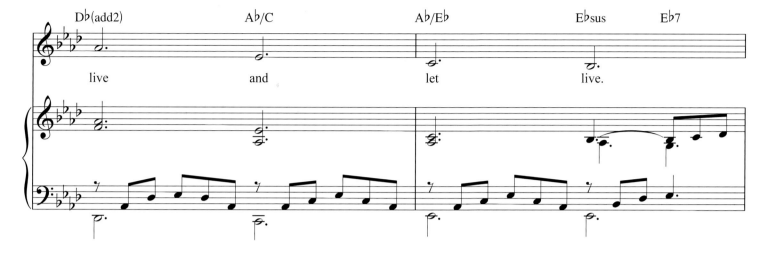

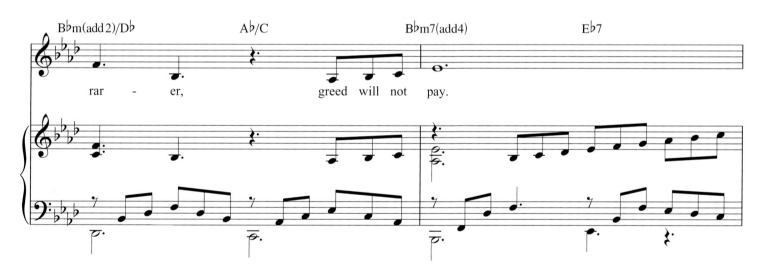

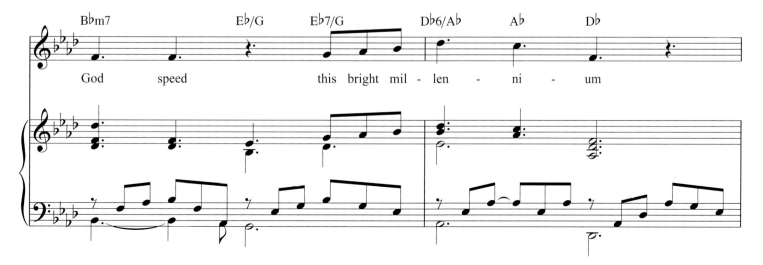

on its way. Let it come some-day.

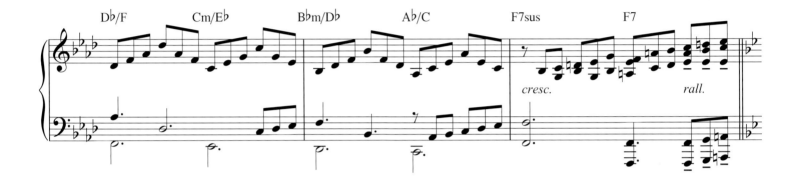

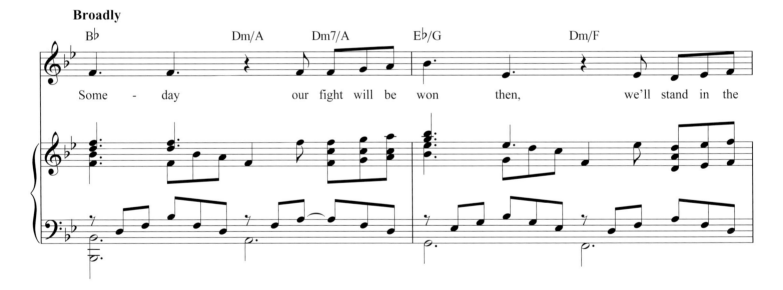

Broadly

Some-day our fight will be won then, we'll stand in the

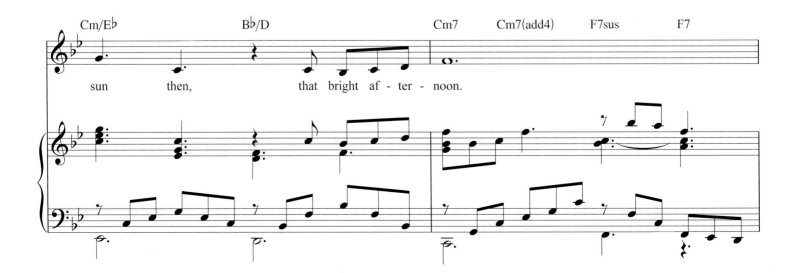

sun then, that bright af-ter-noon.

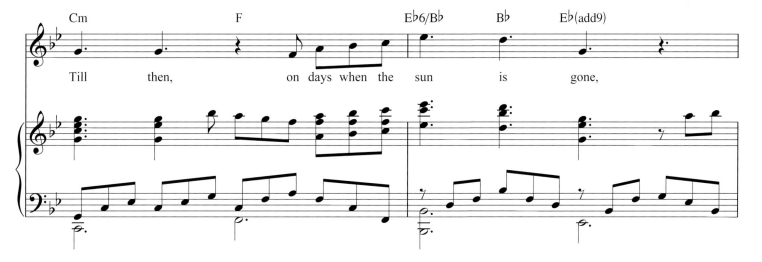

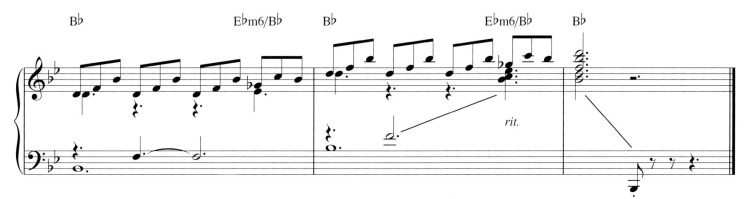

Go the Distance

From *HERCULES*

Music by ALAN MENKEN
Lyrics by DAVID ZIPPEL

Slowly

I have of-ten dreamed of a far-off place, where a
un-known road to em-brace my fate, where a thought that

he-ro's wel-come would be wait-ing for me, where the crowds will cheer when they
road may wan-der, it will lead me to you. And a thou-sand years would be

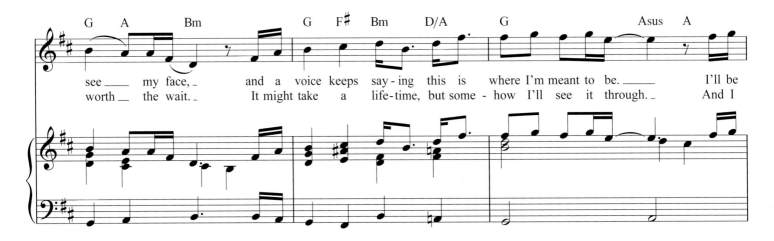

see my face, and a voice keeps say-ing this is where I'm meant to be. I'll be
worth the wait. It might take a life-time, but some-how I'll see it through. And I

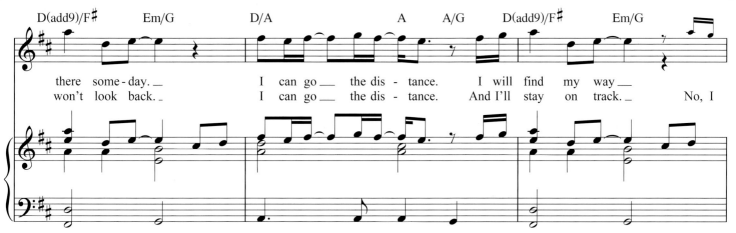

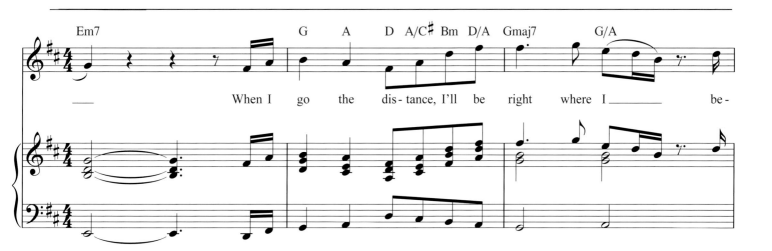

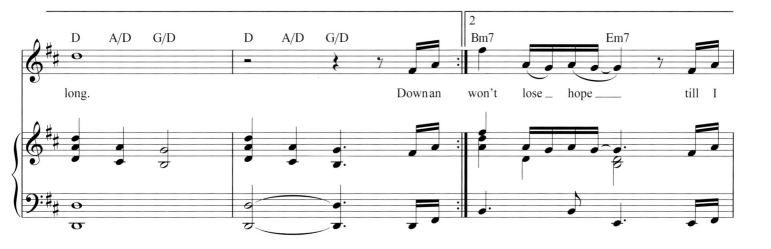

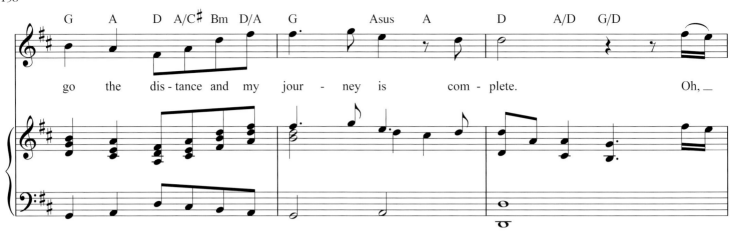

go the dis - tance and my jour - ney is com - plete. Oh, __

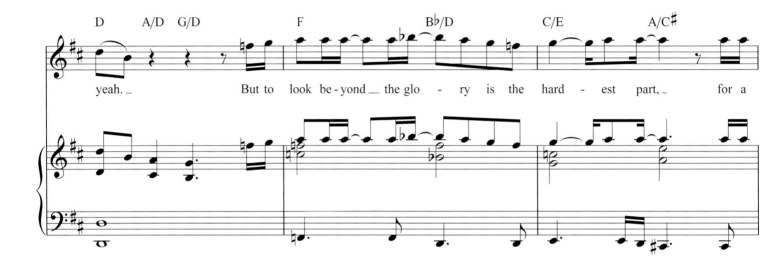

yeah. __ But to look be - yond __ the glo - ry is the hard - est part, __ for a

he - ro's strength __ is meas - ured by his heart.

Like a

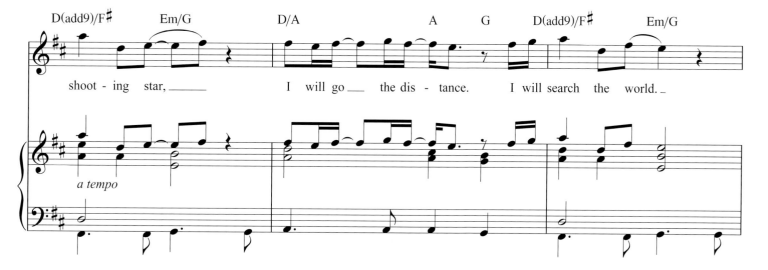

shoot - ing star,_____ I will go__ the dis - tance. I will search the world.__

I will face__ its harms. I_____ don't care how far._____ I can go the dis - tance till I

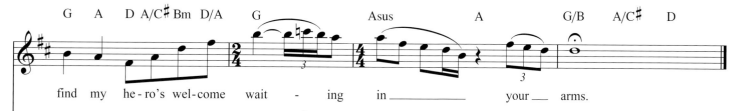

find my he - ro's wel-come wait - ing in _____ your __ arms.

Reflection

From *MULAN*

Music by MATTHEW WILDER
Lyrics by DAVID ZIPPEL

Moderately slow

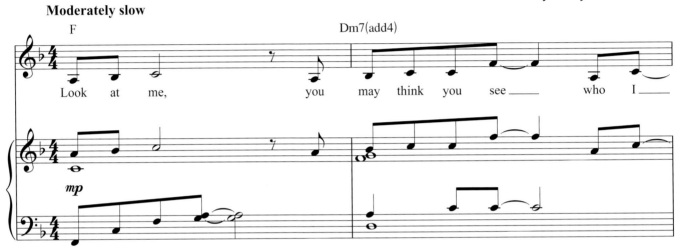

Look at me, you may think you see ___ who I ___

___ real - ly am, ___ but you'll nev - er know me. Ev - 'ry day it's

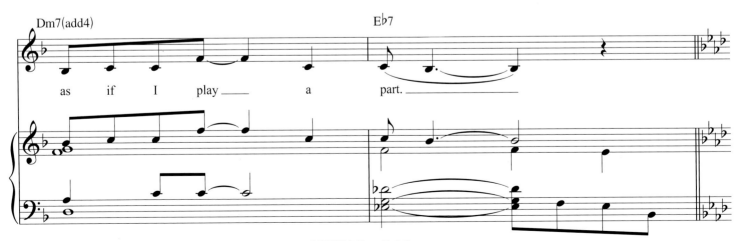

as if I play ___ a part. ___

Now I see / But some-how   if I / I will   wear a mask / show the world   I can / what's in -

fool   the world, / side   my heart   but I can-not / and be loved for   fool my _____ heart. / who I _____ am.

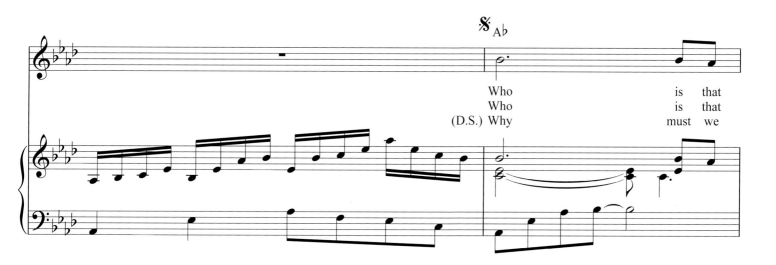

Who   is that / Who   is that / (D.S.) Why   must we

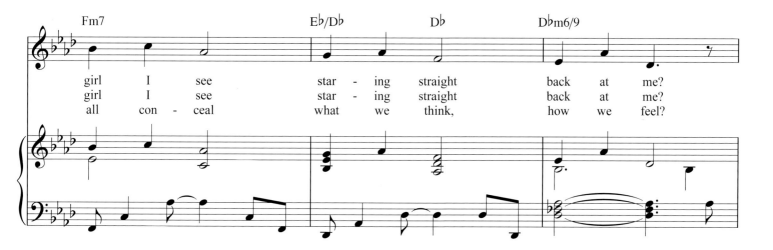

girl I see   star - ing straight   back at me? / girl I see   star - ing straight   back at me? / all con - ceal   what we think,   how we feel?

When will my re - flec - tion show   who I am in -
Why is my re - flec - tion some - one
Must there be a se - cret me I'm

side?   I am now   in a

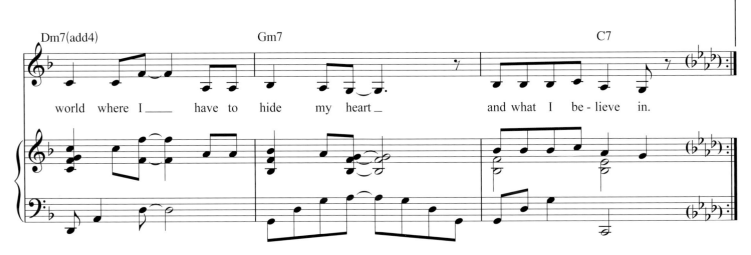

world where I ___ have to hide my heart ___ and what I be - lieve in.

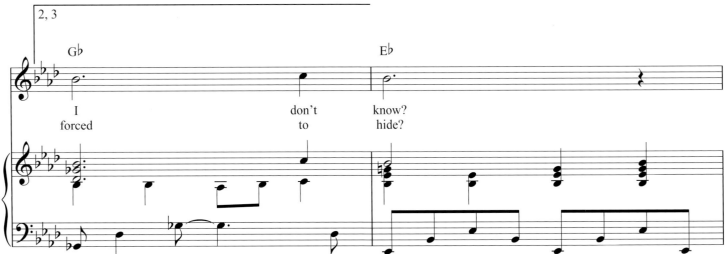

I   don't   know?
forced   to   hide?

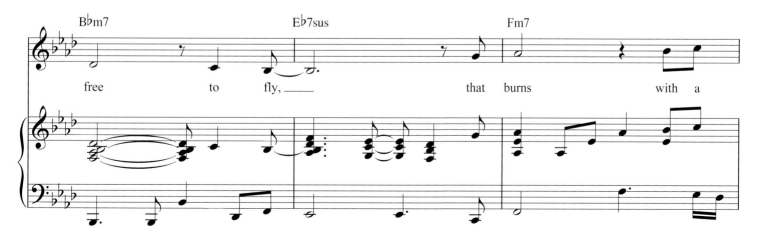

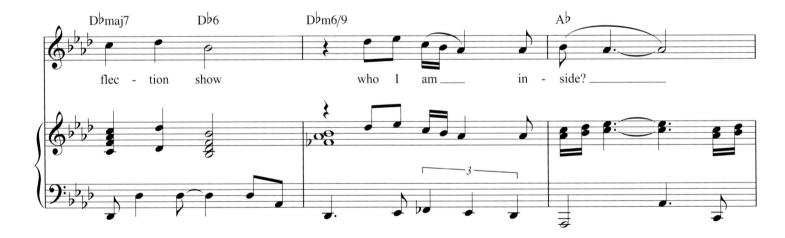

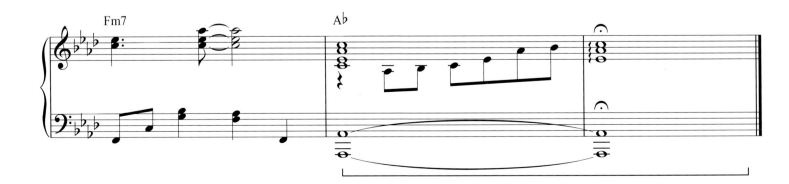

You'll Be in My Heart
(Pop Version)

From *TARZAN*™

Words and Music by
PHIL COLLINS

Moderately

Come stop your cry-ing; _ it will be all right. Just take my hand,

hold it tight. _____ I will pro-tect you from all a-round_ you.

I will be here; don't you _____ cry.

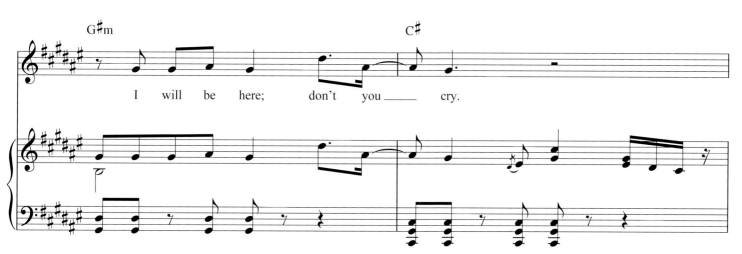

For one so small you seem so ___ strong. ___ My arms will hold you, ___ keep you
Why can't they un-der-stand the way we ___ feel? ___ They just don't trust ___ what they

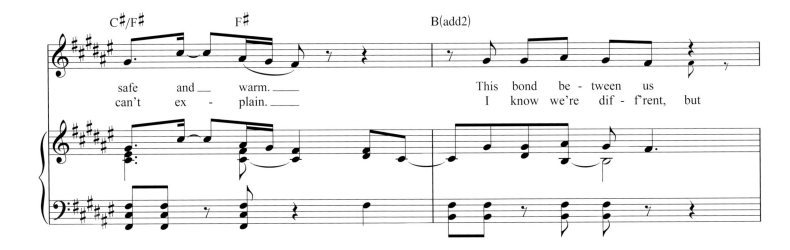

safe and ___ warm. ___ This bond be - tween us
can't ex - plain. ___ I know we're dif - f'rent, but

can't be bro - ken. I will be here; don't you ___ cry. 'Cause
deep in - side us we're not that dif - fer - ent at all. ___ And

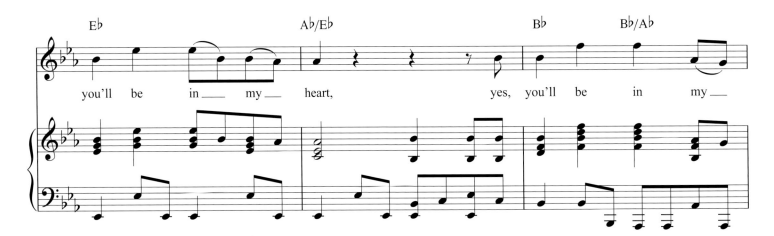

you'll be in ___ my ___ heart, yes, you'll be in my ___

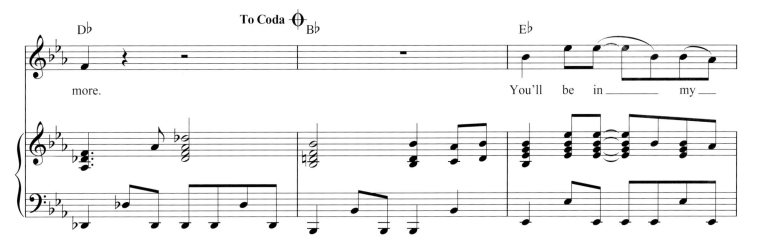

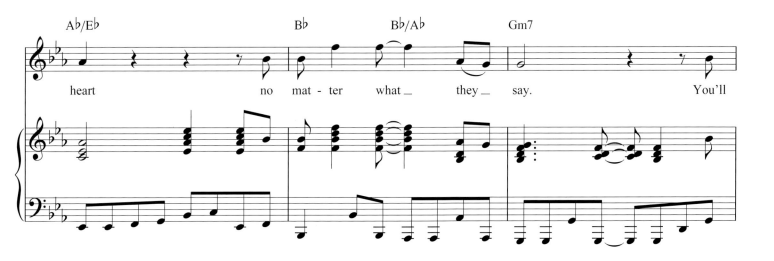

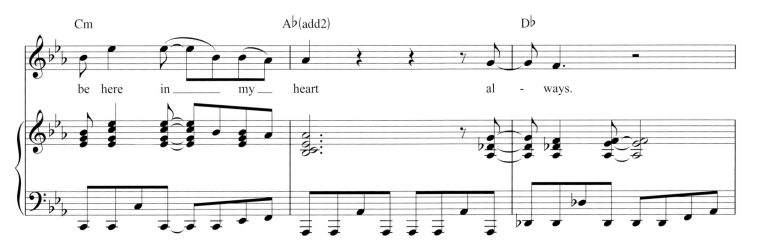

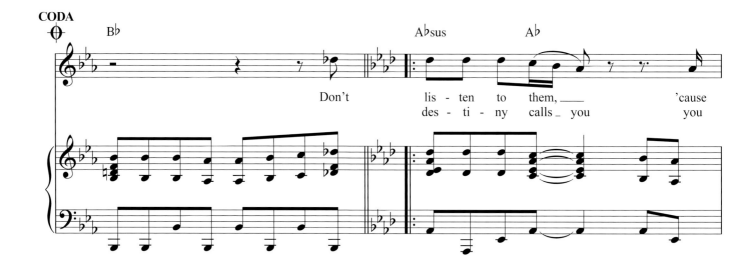

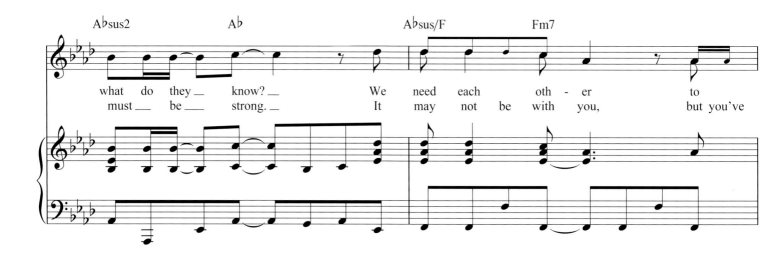

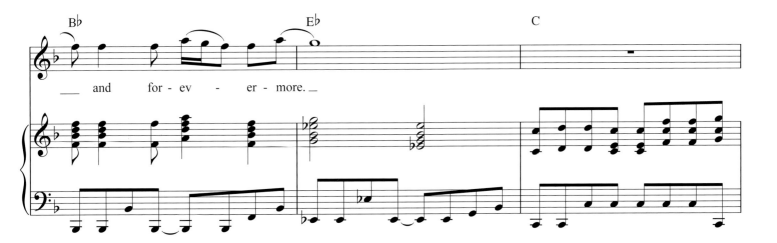

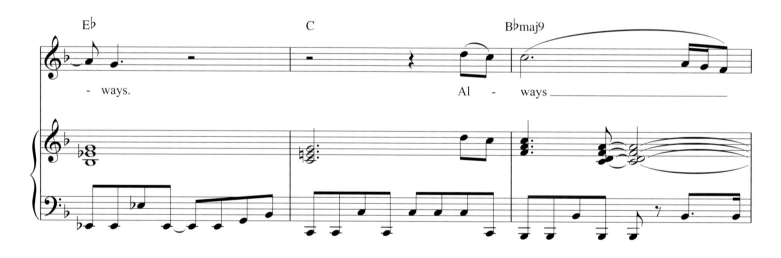

there for __ you al - ways, al - ways __ and al - ways. __

Just look o - ver your shoul - der. Just look o -

- ver your shoul - der. Just look o - ver your shoul - der;

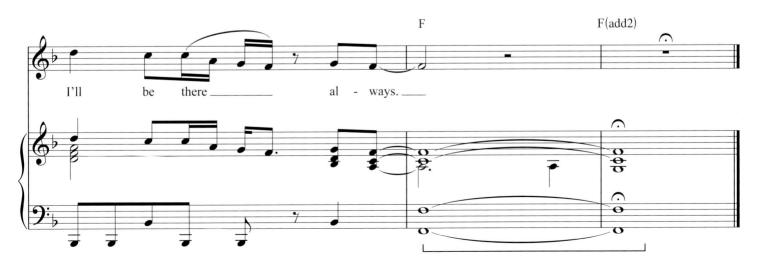

I'll be there _____ al - ways. __

When She Loved Me

From *TOY STORY 2*

Music and Lyrics by
RANDY NEWMAN

Tenderly, very freely

When some - bod - y loved me, ev - 'ry - thing was beau - ti - ful.

Ev - 'ry hour we spent to - geth - er lives with - in my heart.

And when she was sad, I was there to dry her tears; and when she was hap - py, so __ was

174

Written in the Stars

From *AIDA*

Music by ELTON JOHN
Lyrics by TIM RICE

Moderately slow

Male: I am here to tell you we can nev-er meet a-gain. Sim-ple real-ly, is-n't it? A

word or two and then a life time of not know-ing where or how or why or when. You

think of me or speak of me or won-der what be-fell the some-one you once loved so long a-

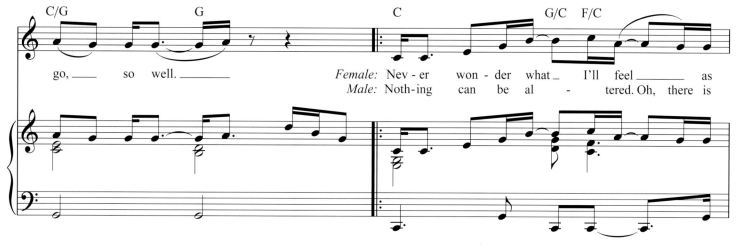

go, ___ so well. ___
Female: Nev-er won-der what __ I'll feel ___ as
Male: Noth-ing can be al - tered. Oh, there is

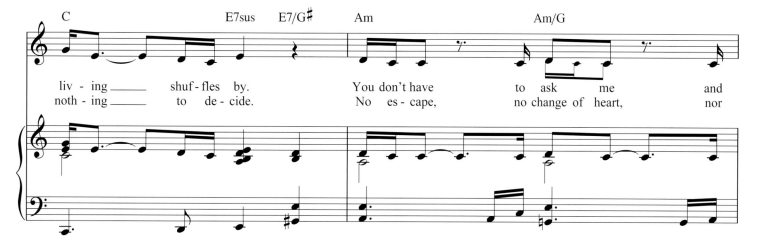

liv - ing ___ shuf-fles by. You don't have to ask me and
noth - ing ___ to de - cide. No es - cape, no change of heart, nor

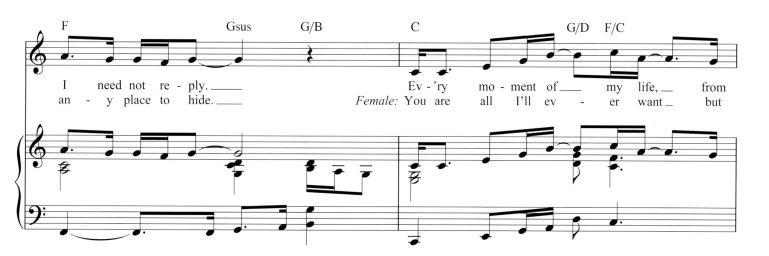

I need not re - ply. ___ Ev - 'ry mo - ment of ___ my life, __ from
an - y place to hide. ___ *Female:* You are all I'll ev - er want __ but

now un - til I die, ___ I will think or dream of you and
this I am de - nied. __ Some-times in my dark - est thoughts I

fail _____ to un-der-stand how a per-fect love __ can be con-found - ed
wish _____ I nev - er learned what it is to be __ in love and have that

out of hand. _____ } *Both:* Is it writ - ten in the stars? ___ Are we
love re - turned. _____

pay - ing for some crime? _ Is that all that we are good for, __ just a

stretch of mor - tal time? _____ Is this God's ex - per - i - ment ___ in

which we have＿ no say?＿ In which we're giv-en par-a-dise, but

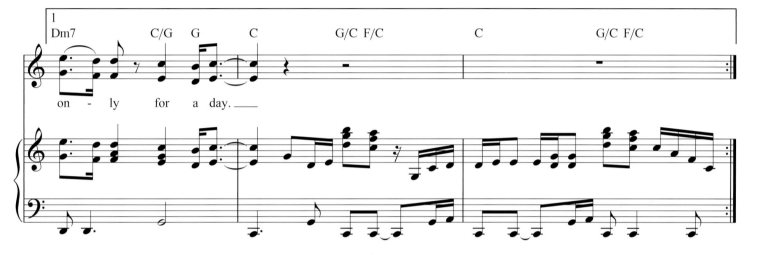

on - ly for a day.＿

on - ly for a day.＿＿ *Male:* Is it writ-ten in the stars?＿ Are we

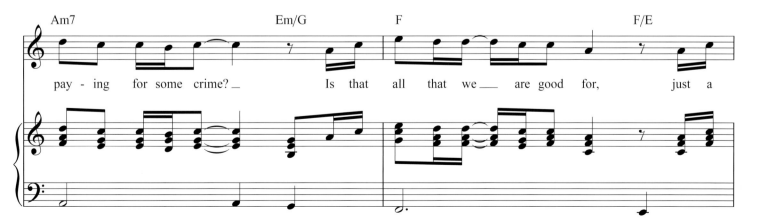

pay-ing for some crime?＿ Is that all that we＿ are good for, just a

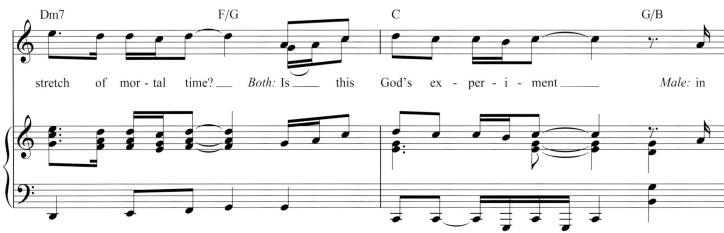

stretch of mor-tal time?___ *Both:* Is___ this God's ex - per - i - ment___ *Male:* in

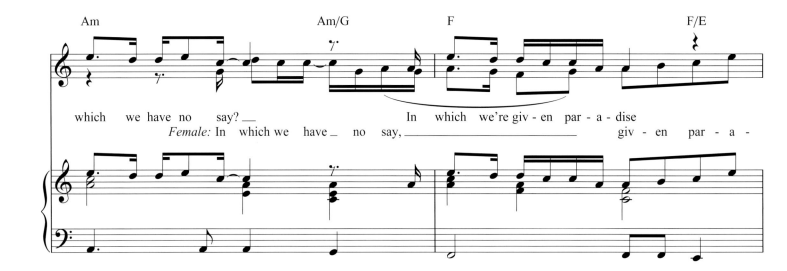

which we have no say?___ In which we're giv-en par-a-dise
Female: In which we have___ no say,_____ giv-en par-a-

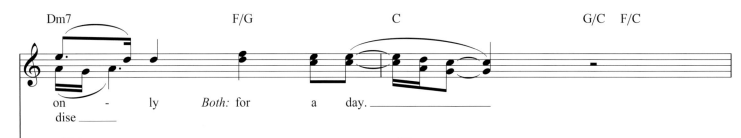

on - ly *Both:* for a day._____
dise_____

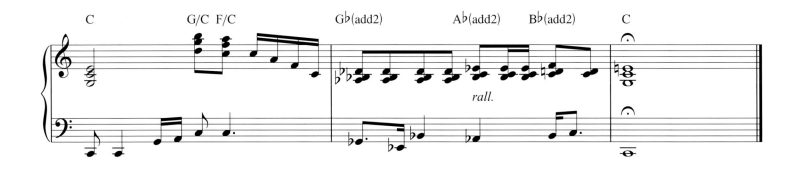

rall.

If I Didn't Have You

From *MONSTERS, INC.*

Music and Lyrics by
RANDY NEWMAN

Sulley: If I were a rich man with a mil-lion or two

Mike: I'd live in a pent - house in a

room with a view. *Sulley:* And if I were hand-

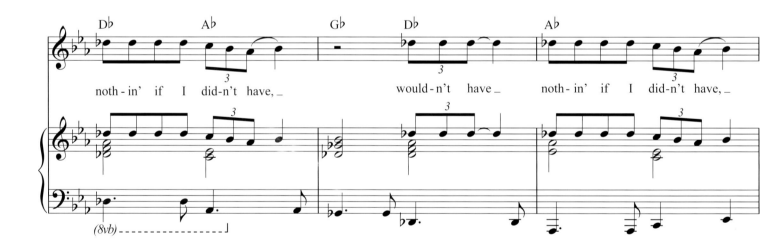

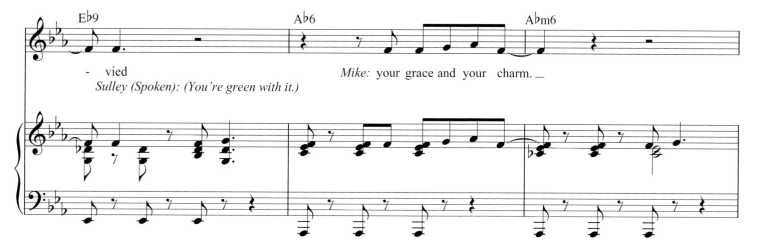

-vied

Mike: your grace and your charm. _

Sulley (Spoken): (You're green with it.)

Ev-'ry-one loves _ you, _ you know. _ Sulley: Yes, I

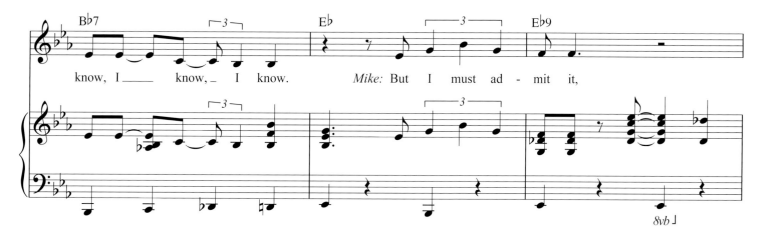

know, I _ know, _ I know. Mike: But I must ad-mit it,

8vb

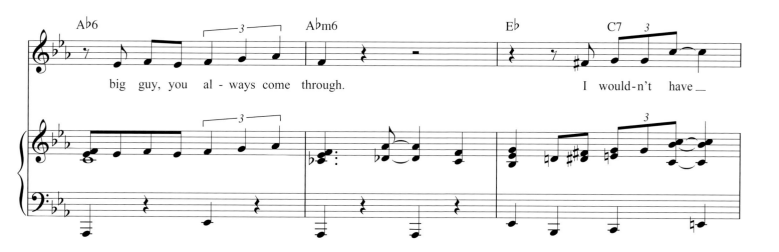

big guy, you al-ways come through. I would-n't have _

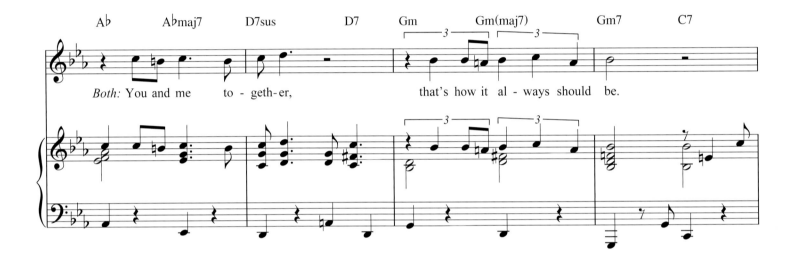

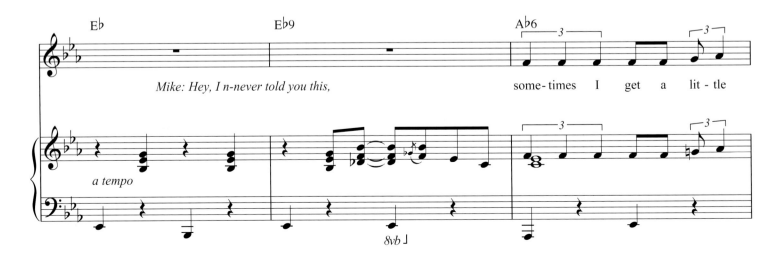

185

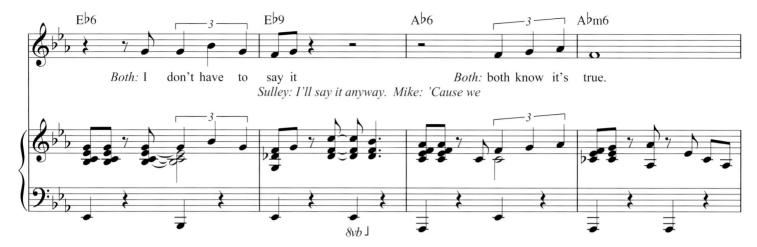

Both: I don't have to say it   Both: both know it's true.
Sulley: I'll say it anyway. Mike: 'Cause we

I would-n't have __ noth-in' if I did-n't have, __   I would-n't have __

noth-in' if I did-n't have, __   I would-n't have __   noth-in' if I did-n't have __

Much slower

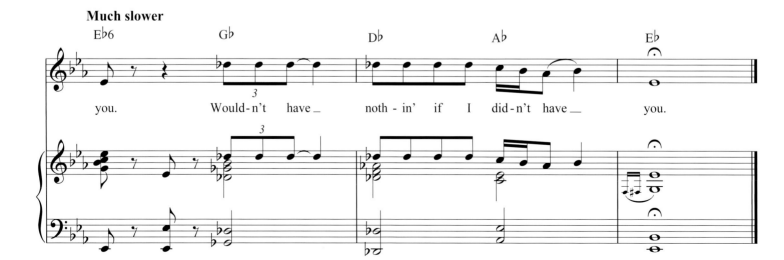

you.   Would-n't have __ noth - in' if I did-n't have __   you.

If I Didn't Have You

From *MONSTERS, INC.*

Music and Lyrics by Randy Newman

Sulley:	If I were a rich man with a million or two
Mike:	I'd live in a penthouse in a room with a view
Sulley:	And if I were handsome
Mike:	*No way!*
Sulley:	*It could happen.*
	'Cause dreams do come true
	I woudn't have nothin' if I didn't have you
	Woudn't have nothin' if I didn't have
	Wouldn't have nothin' if I didn't have
	Wouldn't have nothin'
Mike:	*Can I tell you something?*
	For years I have envied
Sulley:	*You're green with it.*
Mike:	Your grace and your charm
	Everyone loves you, you know
Sulley:	Yes, I know, I know, I know
Mike:	But I must admit it, big guy, you always come through
	I wouldn't have nothing if I didn't have you
Both:	You and me together, that's how it always should be
	One without the other don't mean nothing to me, nothing to me
Mike:	*Yeah, I wouldn't be nothing, if I didn't have you to serve.*
	I'm just a punky little eyeball and a funky optic nerve
	Hey, I never told you this.
	Sometimes I get a little blue
Sulley:	*Looks good on you.*
Mike:	But I wouldn't have nothing if I didn't have you
Sulley:	*Let's dance!*
Mike:	*Look, Ma, I'm dancing! Would you let me lead?*
	Look at that! It's true! Big guys are light on their feet.
	Don't you dare dip me. Don't you dare dip me.
	Don't you dare dip me. Ow! I should have stretched.
Sulley:	Yes, I wouldn't be nothin' if I didn't have you
Mike:	*I know what you mean, Sulley, because...*
Sulley:	I wouldn't know where to go
Mike:	*Me too, because I...*
Sulley:	Wouldn't know what to do
Mike:	*Why do you keep singing my part?*
Both:	I don't have to say it
Sulley:	*I'll say it anyway.*
Mike:	'Cause we...
Both:	...both know it's true
	I wouldn't have nothin' if I didn't have
	I wouldn't have nothin' if I didn't have
	I wouldn't have nothin' if I didn't have
	Wouldn't have nothin' if I didn't have you
Mike:	*One more time. It worked!*
Sulley:	Don't have to say it
Mike:	*Where'd everybody come from?*
Sulley:	'Cause we both know it's true
Mike:	*Let's take it home, big guy!*
Both:	I wouldn't have nothin' if I didn't have
	I wouldn't have nothin' if I didn't have
	I wouldn't have nothin, if I didn't have...
Mike:	...you. *You. You. A, E, I, O,*
Sulley:	*That means you. Yeah!*

The Medallion Calls

From *PIRATES OF THE CARIBBEAN:*
THE CURSE OF THE BLACK PEARL

Music by KLAUS BADELT

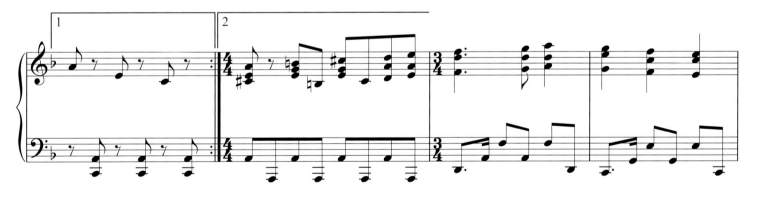

The Incredits

From *THE INCREDIBLES*

Music by MICHAEL GIACCHINO

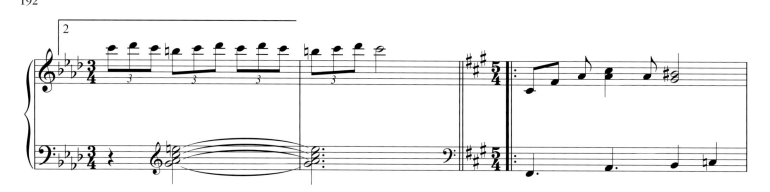

True Love's Kiss

From *ENCHANTED*

Music by ALAN MENKEN
Lyrics by STEPHEN SCHWARTZ

Flowing and free

I've been dream-ing of a true love's kiss; and a prince I'm hop-ing comes with this. That's what brings ev-er - af-ter-ings so hap - py. And that's the rea-son we need lips so much,

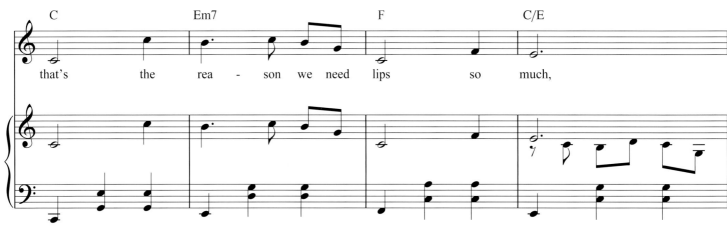

that's the rea - son we need lips so much,

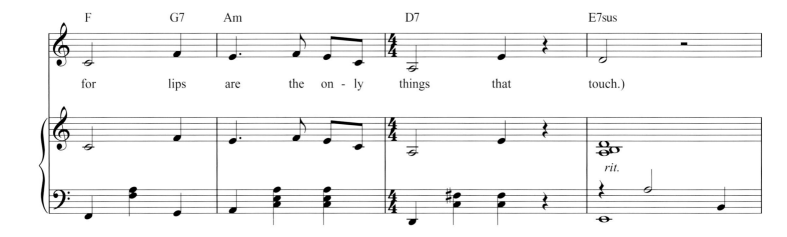

for lips are the on - ly things that touch.)

Flowing

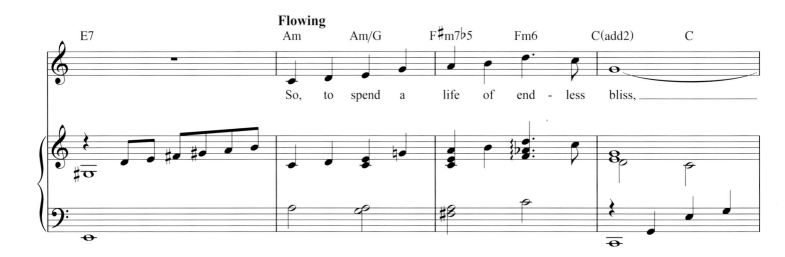

So, to spend a life of end - less bliss, _____

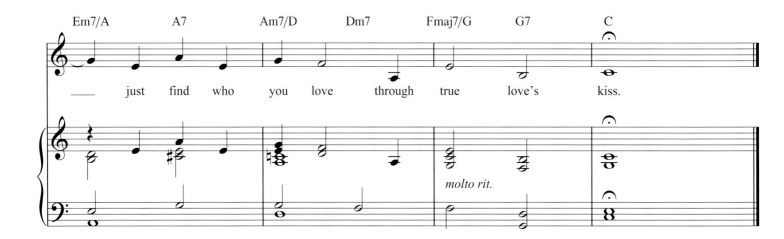

_____ just find who you love through true love's kiss.

Married Life

From *UP*

By MICHAEL GIACCHINO

Moderately fast

mp

With light pedal

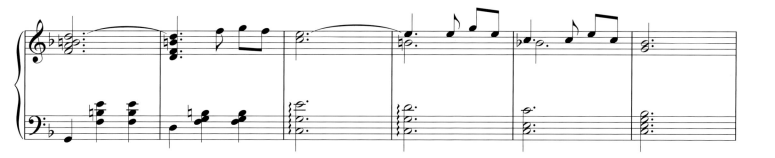

cresc.

mf

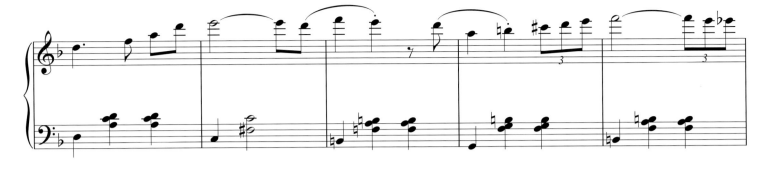

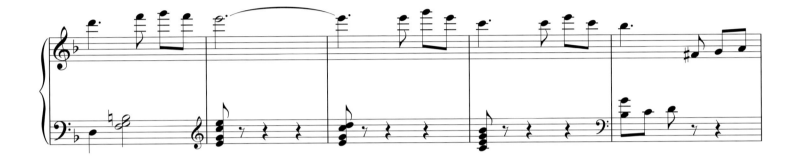

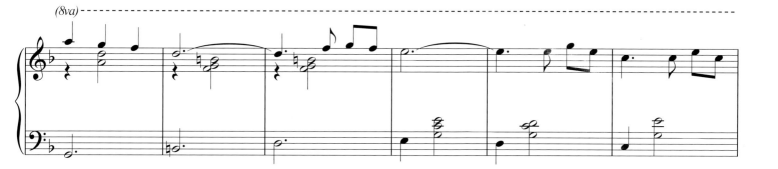

Deliberately   **Tempo I**

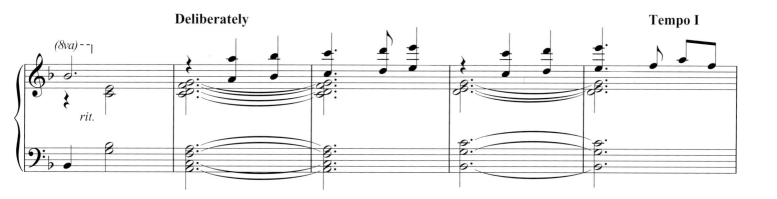

Wistful

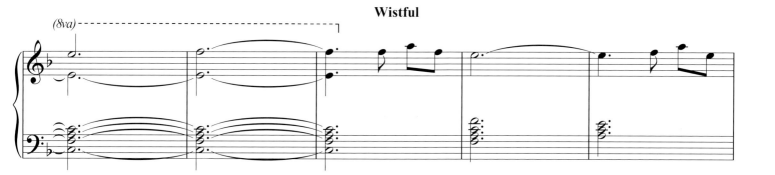

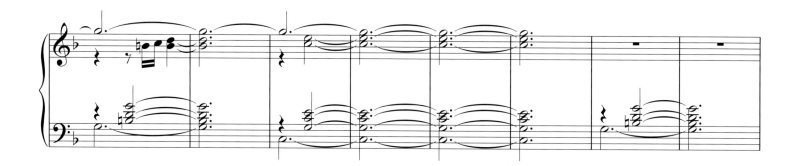

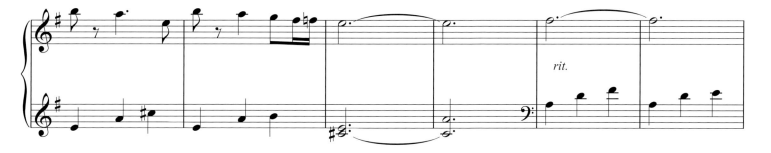

Slower

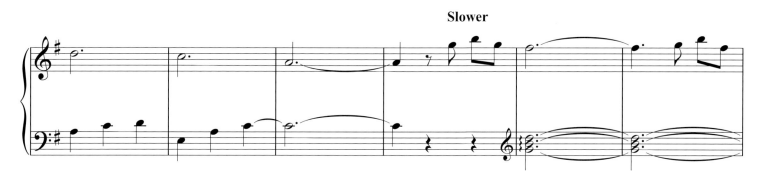

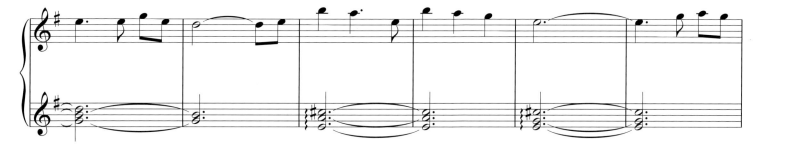

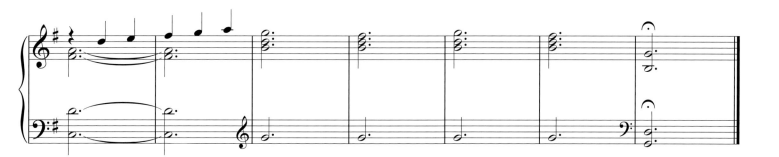

Almost There

From *THE PRINCESS AND THE FROG*

Music and Lyrics by
RANDY NEWMAN

Moderately, expressively

That's just gon-na have to wait a while. _ Ain't got time for

mess-in' a-round, _ and it's not my style. ____

This old town _ can slow you down, peo-ple tak-in' the eas - y way, but

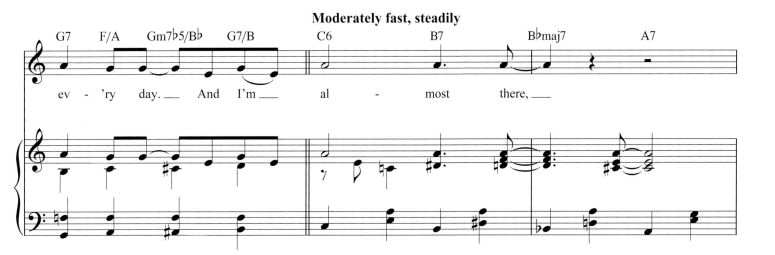

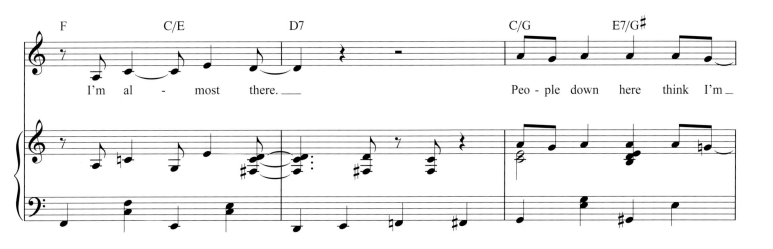

Trials _____ and trib-u-la - tions, I've had __ my share. __

__ There ain't noth - ing gon - na stop me now __ 'cause I'm __

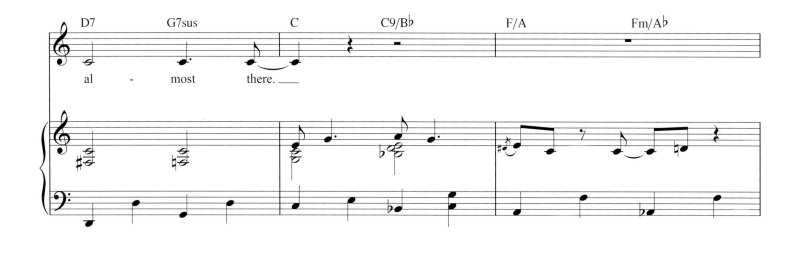

al - most there. __

I re - mem - ber Dad - dy told __

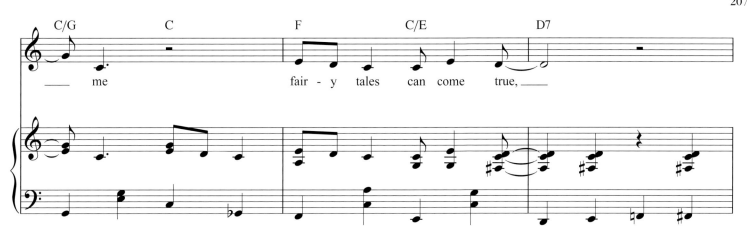

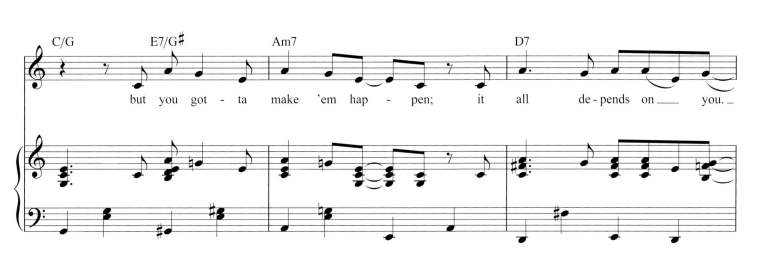

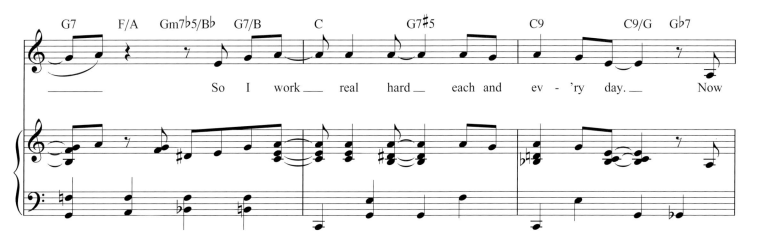

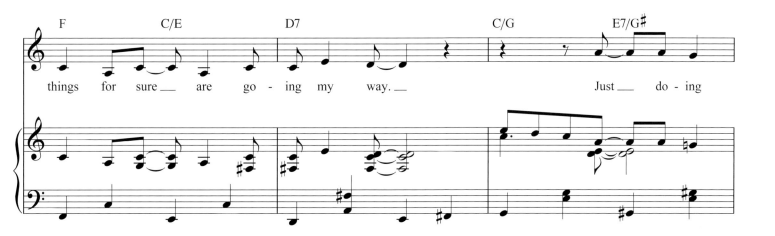

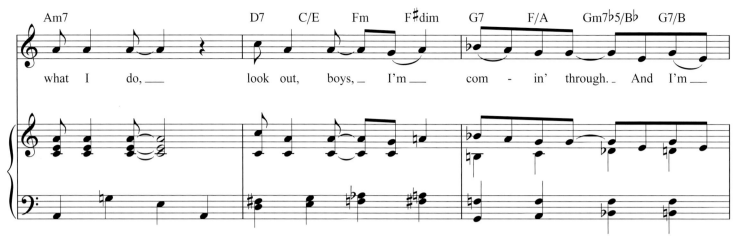

what I do, ___ look out, boys, _ I'm __ com - in' through. _ And I'm __

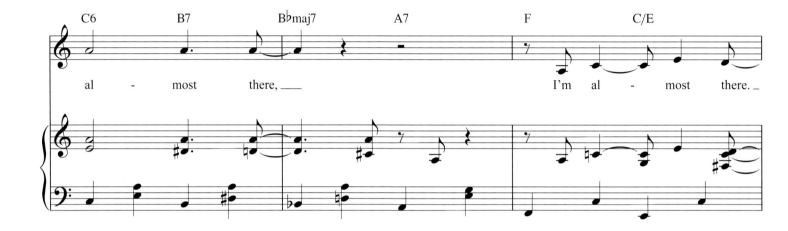

al - most there, ___ I'm al - most there. __

___ Peo - ple gon - na come here from ev - 'ry - where, _ and I'm

al - most there, ___ I'm al - most there. __

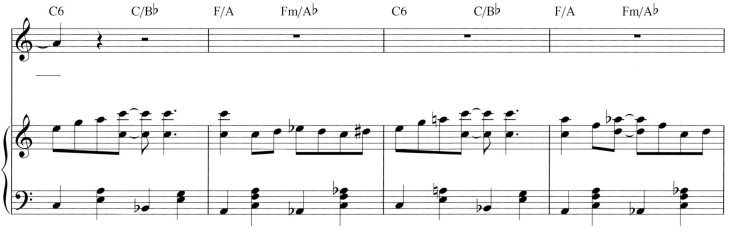

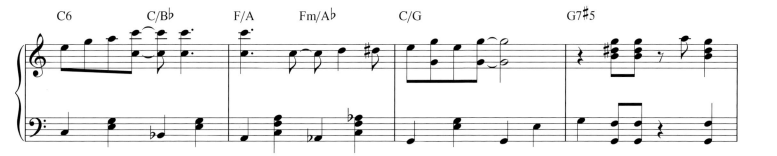

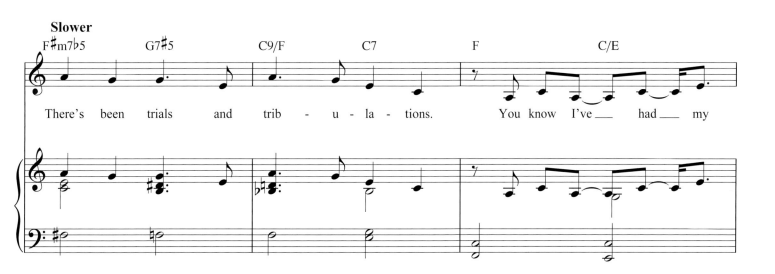

There's been trials and trib - u - la - tions. You know I've__ had __ my

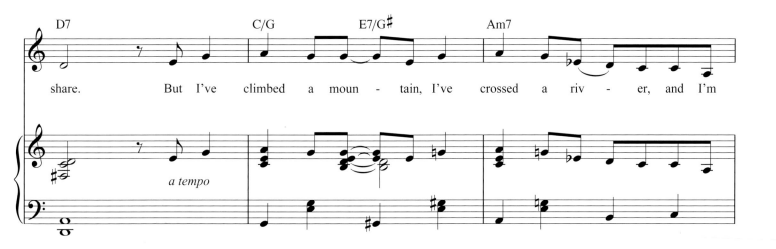

share. But I've climbed a moun - tain, I've crossed a riv - er, and I'm

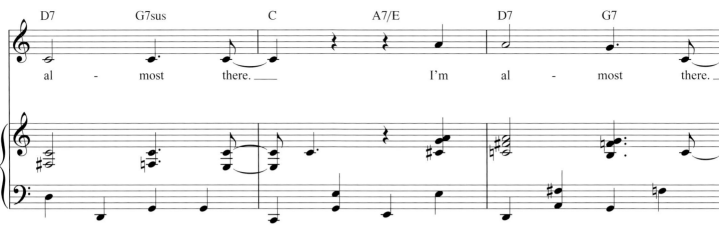

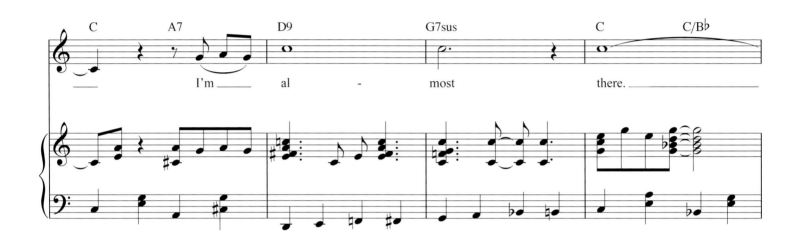

I See the Light

From *TANGLED*

Music by ALAN MENKEN
Lyrics by GLENN SLATER

Female: All those days, watch-ing from the win-dows.
Now I'm here, blink-ing in the star-light.

All those years, out-side, look-ing in.
Now I'm here; sud-den - ly I see.

All that time, nev - er e - ven know-ing just how blind I've been.

warm and real and bright, and the world has some - how

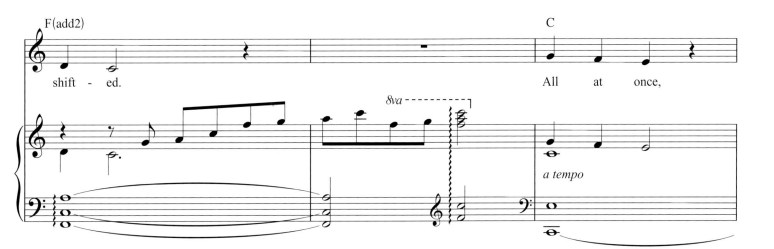

shift - ed. All at once,

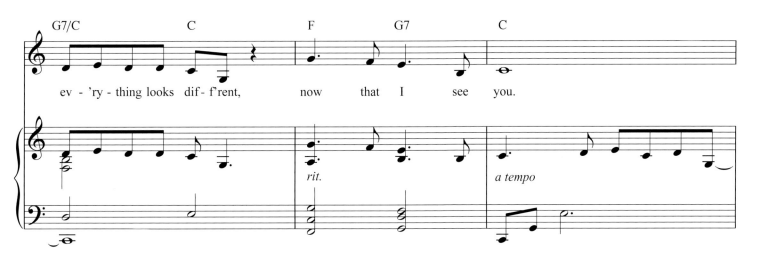

ev - 'ry - thing looks dif - f'rent, now that I see you.

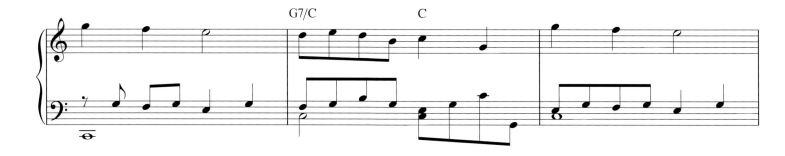

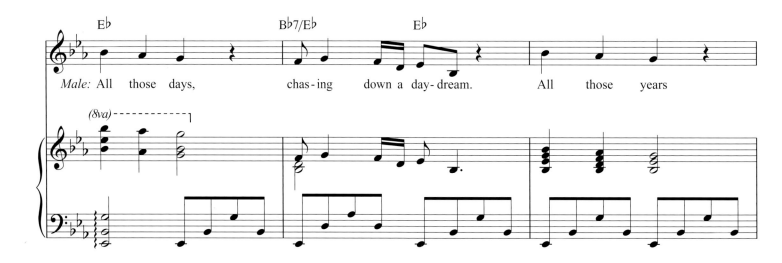

Male: All those days, chas-ing down a day- dream. All those years

215

liv-ing in a blur. All that time, nev-er tru-ly see-ing

things the way they were. Now she's here,

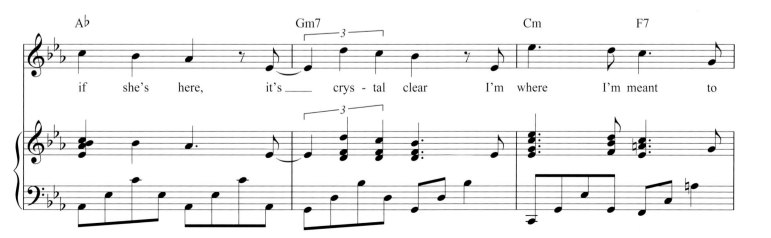

shin-ing in the star-light. Now she's here; sud-den-ly I know:

if she's here, it's___ crys-tal clear I'm where I'm meant to

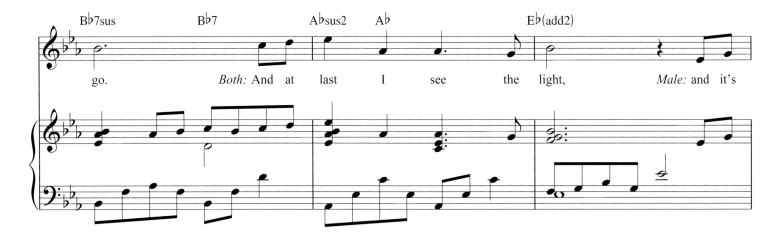

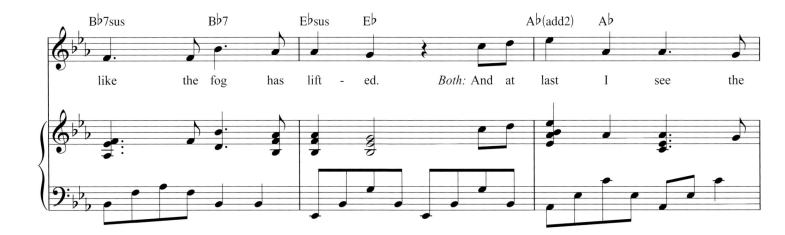

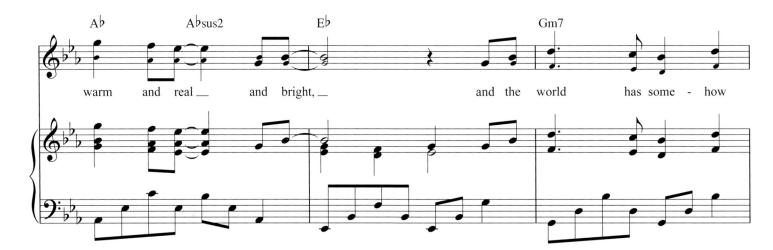

shift - ed. All at once,

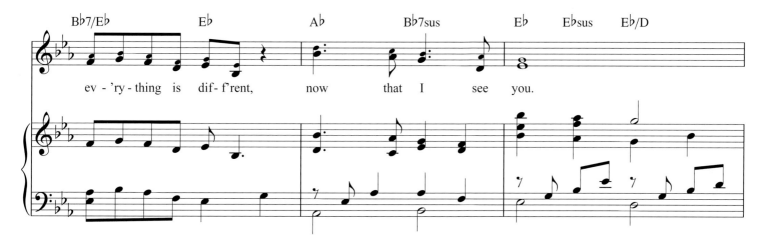

ev - 'ry-thing is dif- f'rent, now that I see you.

Now that I see

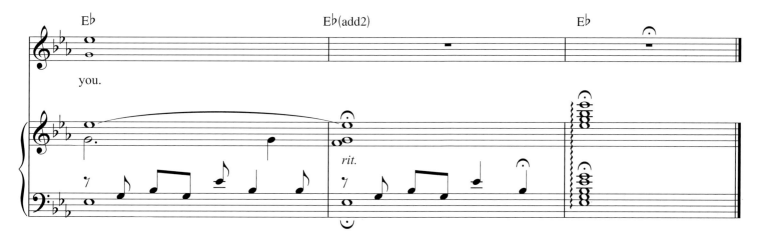

you.

When Will
My Life Begin?

From *TANGLED*

Music by ALAN MENKEN
Lyrics by GLENN SLATER

Moderately fast Rock

Sev - en a. m.,___ the u - su - al morn - ing line - up.
Then af - ter lunch, _ it's puz - zles, and darts and bak - ing...

Start on the chores, _ and sweep _ 'til the floor's all clean.
pa - pier mâ - ché, ___ a bit ___ of bal - let and chess...

Pol - ish and wax, _ do laun - dry, and mop, and shine up.
pot - ter - y and _ ven - tril - o - quy, can - dle - mak - ing...

Sweep a -
then I'll

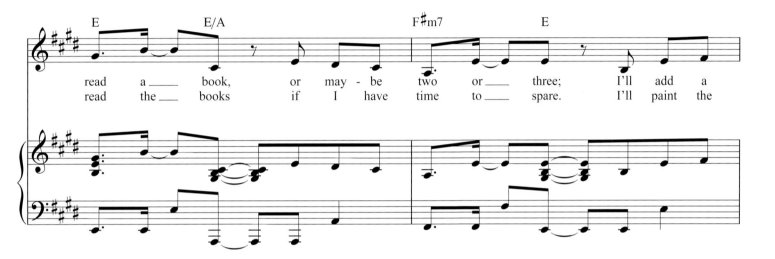

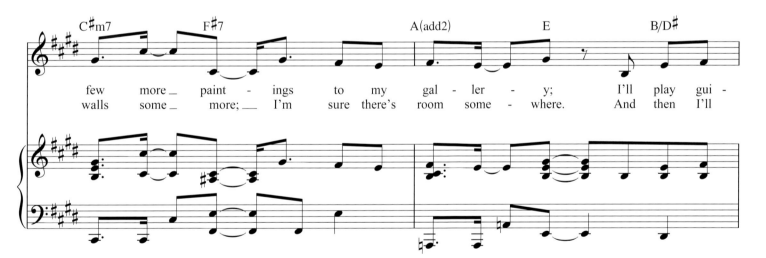

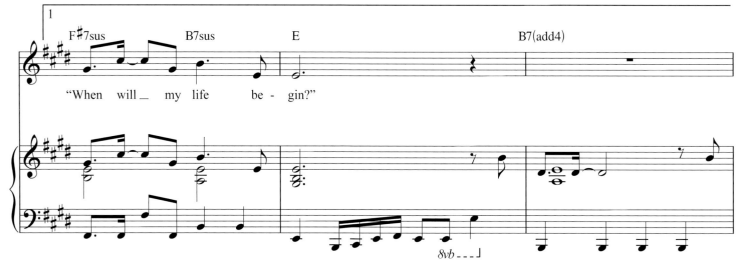

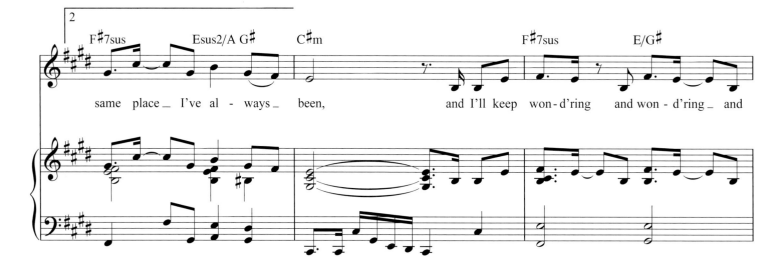

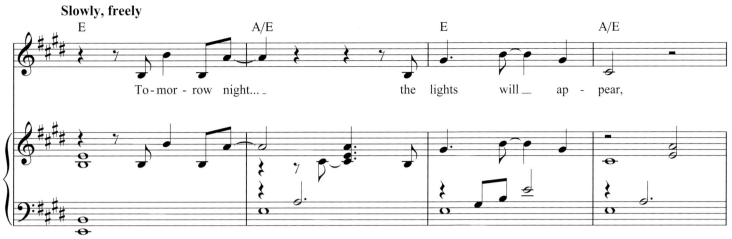

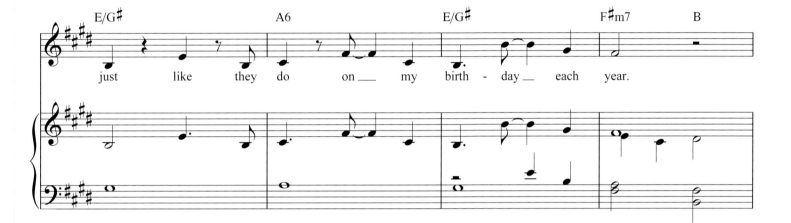

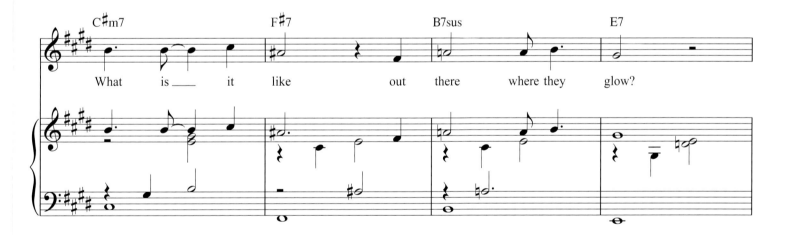

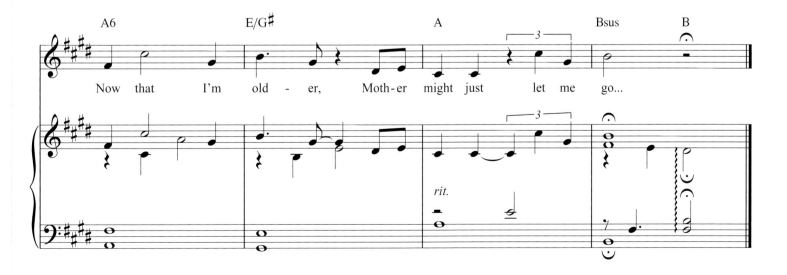

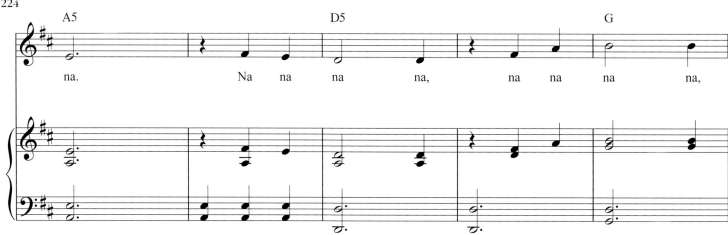

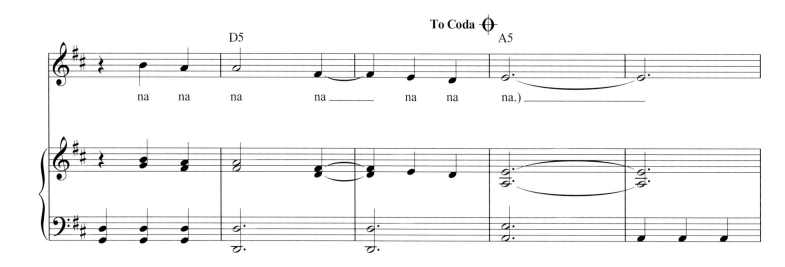

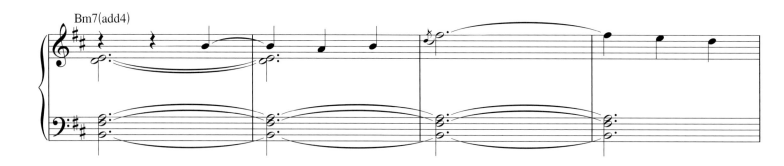

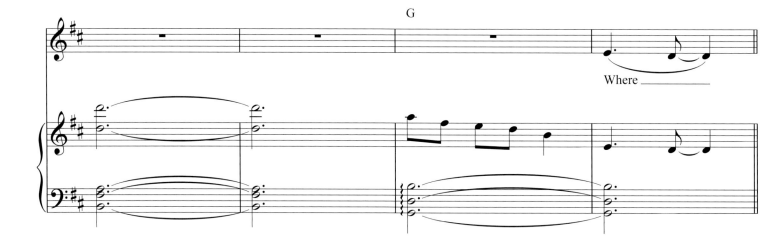

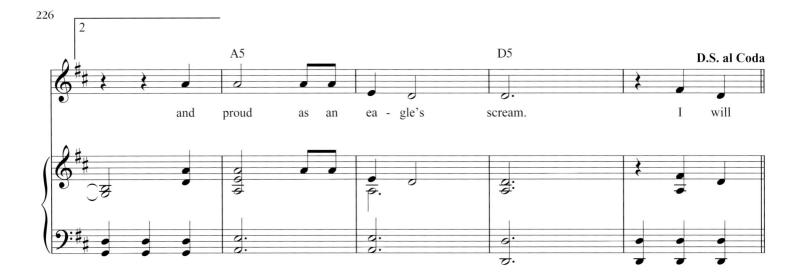

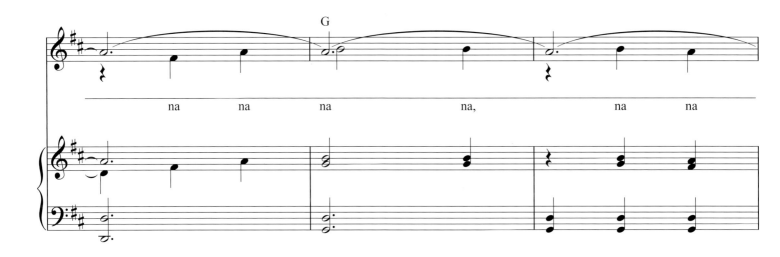

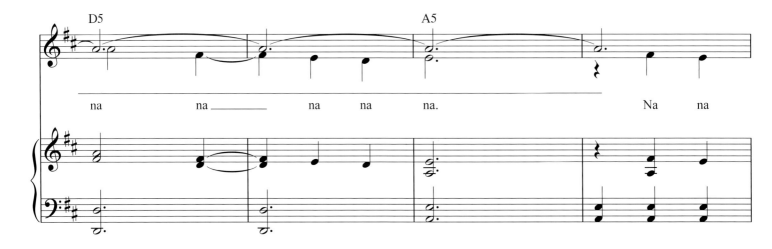

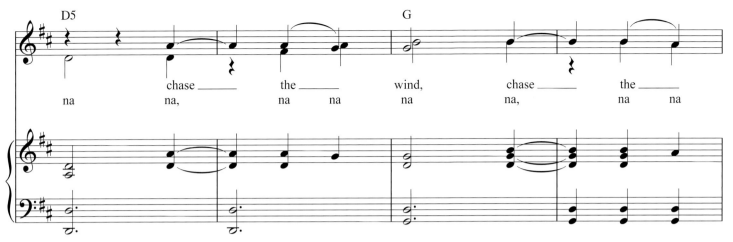

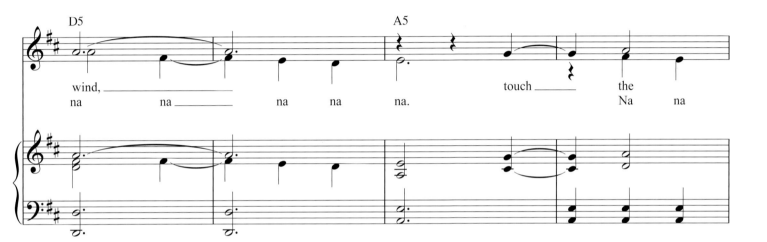

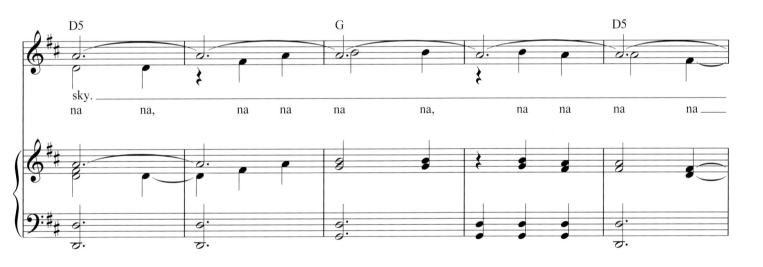

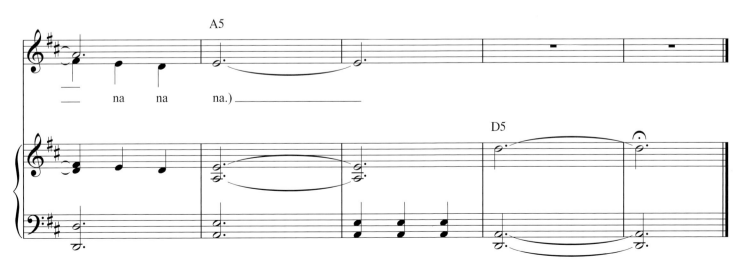

For the First Time in Forever

From *FROZEN*

Music and Lyrics by KRISTEN ANDERSON-LOPEZ
and ROBERT LOPEZ

With excitement

The win-dow is o - pen! So's _ that door! I did-n't know they did that an - y - more. _ Who knew we owned _ eight thou - sand sal - ad plates? For years I've roamed _ these emp - ty halls. _ Why have a ball - room with _ no balls? _

229

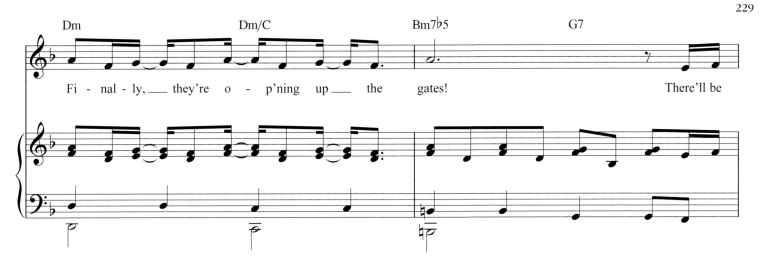

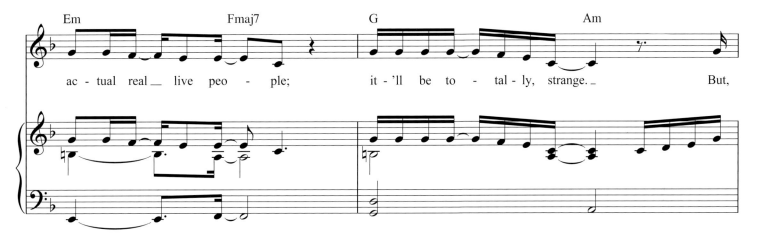

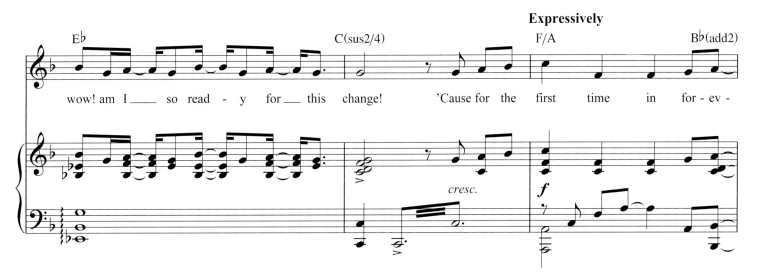

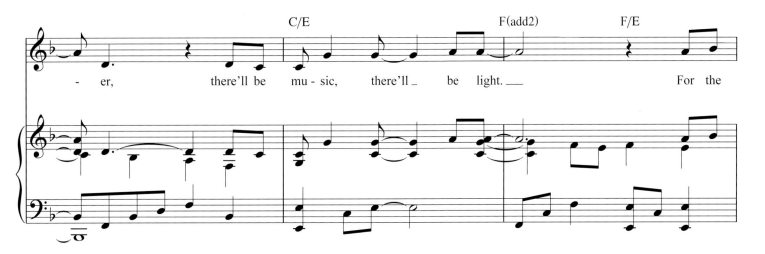

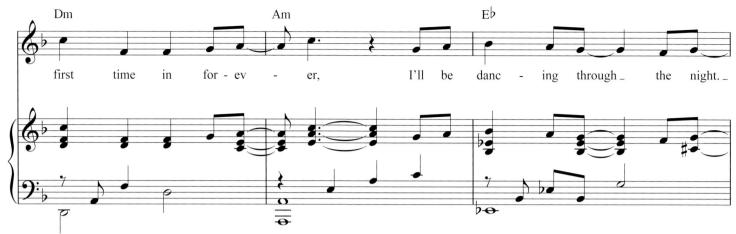

first time in for-ev - er, I'll be danc - ing through __ the night. __

__ Don't know if I'm e - lat - ed or gas - sy, but I'm

some-where in __ that zone. 'Cause for the first time in for - ev -

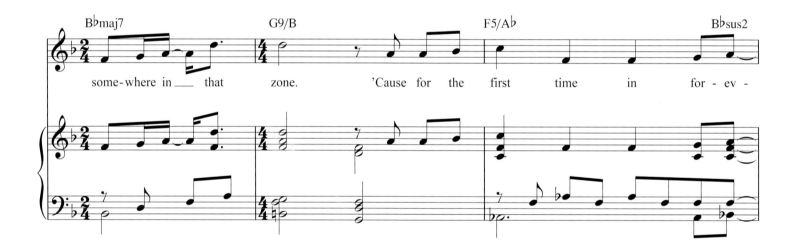

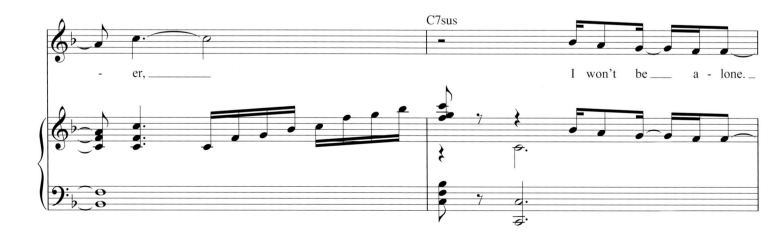

- er, __ I won't be __ a - lone. __

-er, there'll be mag-ic, there'll _ be fun. ___ For the

first time in for-ev-er, I could be no-ticed by ___ some-one. _

And I know it is to-tal-ly cra-zy to

dream I'd find _ ro - mance, but for the first time in for-ev -

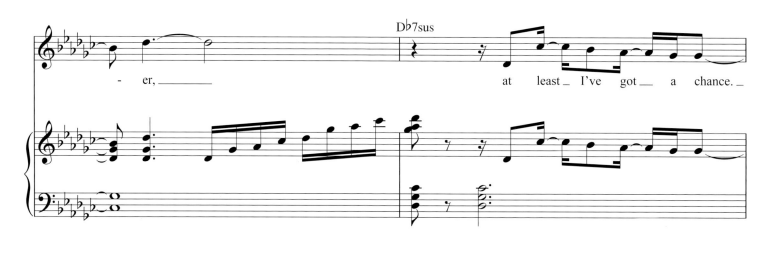

-er, _____ at least _ I've got _ a chance. _

ELSA: Don't let them in; don't let them _ see;

be the good girl _____ you al-ways have to be. _____

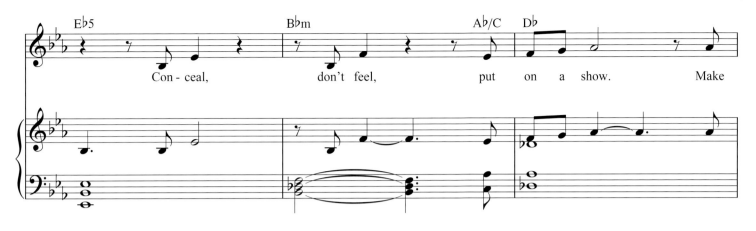

Con - ceal, don't feel, put on a show. Make

one wrong move, and ev - 'ry - one will know.

But it's on - ly for to - day.

ANNA: It's on - ly for to - day! It's ag - o - ny to

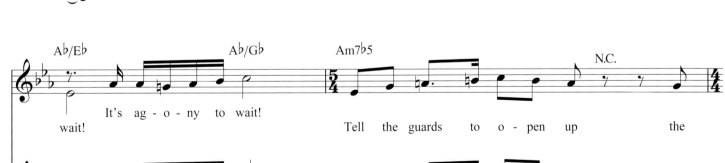

wait! It's ag - o - ny to wait!

Tell the guards to o - pen up the

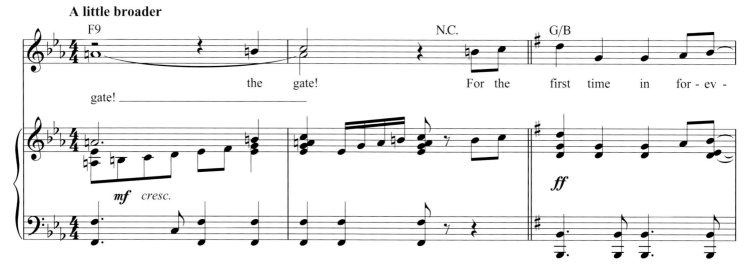

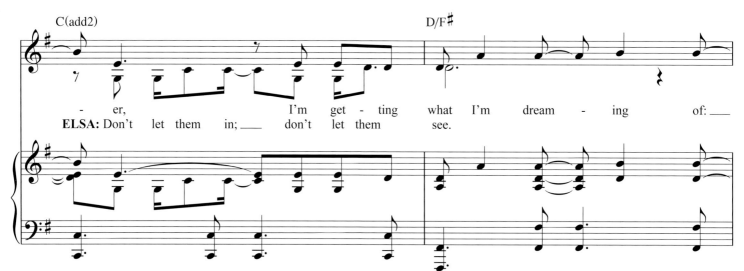

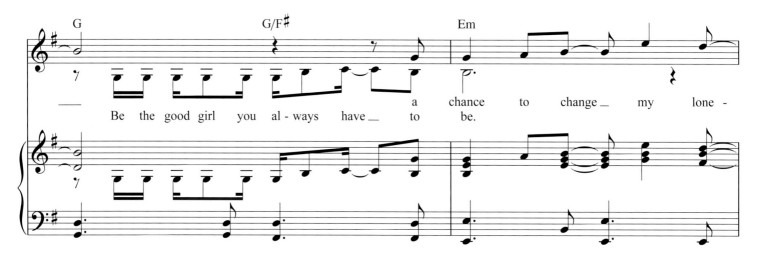

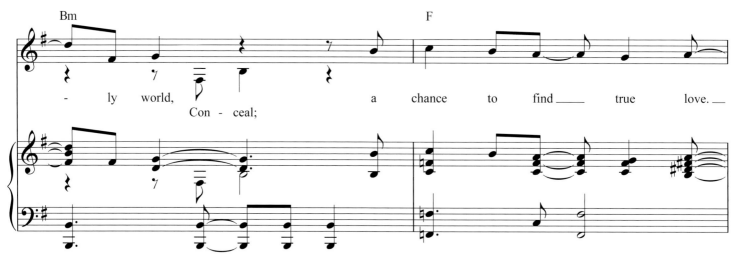

con-ceal, don't feel, don't let them know.   I know it all ends to-mor-row,___ so it

has to be___ to - day.   'Cause for the first time in for-ev -

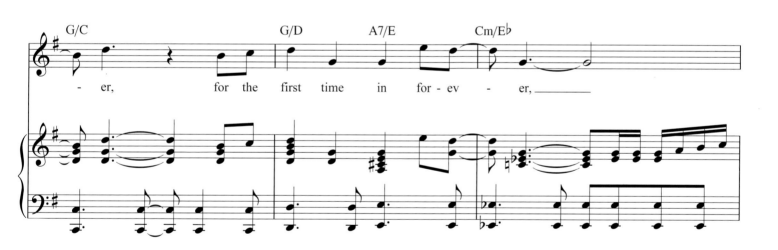

- er,   for the first time in for-ev - er,___

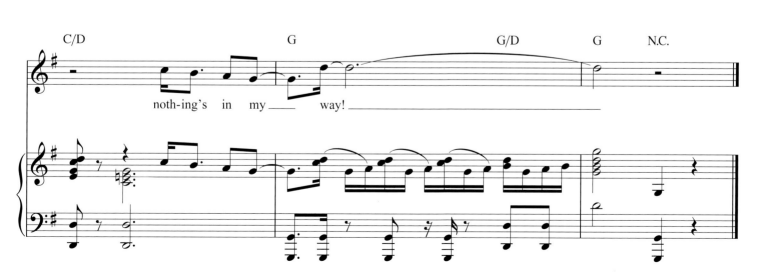

noth-ing's in my___ way!_____________

Let It Go

From *FROZEN*

Music and Lyrics by KRISTEN ANDERSON-LOPEZ
and ROBERT LOPEZ

Half-time feel, mysterious

The snow glows white on the moun-tain to-night;__ not a foot-print ____ to be seen. __

A king-dom of i - so - la - tion, and it

looks like I'm the queen. __ The wind __ is howl - ing like __ this swirl-

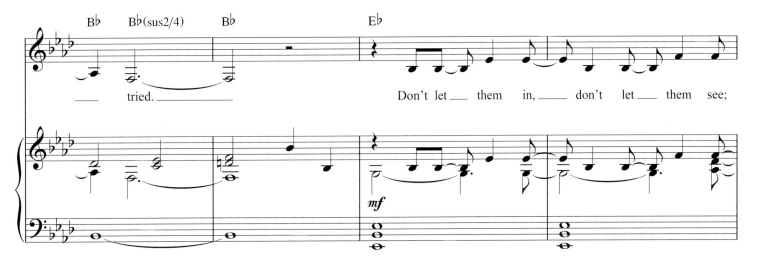

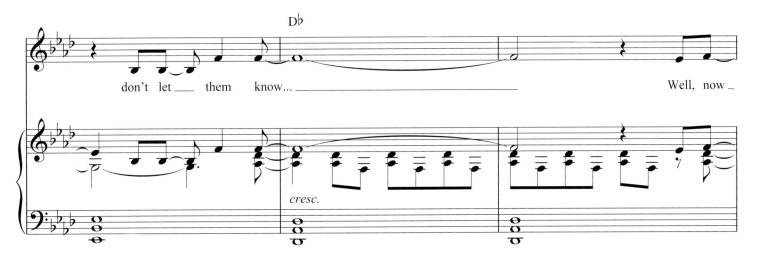

they know. _____ Let it go, ___ let it go; _
let it go; _

— can't __ hold it back an - y - more. __ Let it go, _
— I am one with the wind and sky. ___ Let it go, _

— let it go; ___ turn a - way ___ and slam ___ the _
— let it go; ___ you'll nev - er see ___ me _

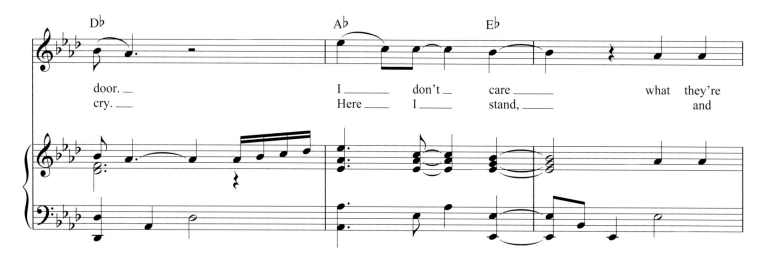

door. _ I ___ don't __ care ___ what they're
cry. __ Here ___ I ___ stand, ___ and

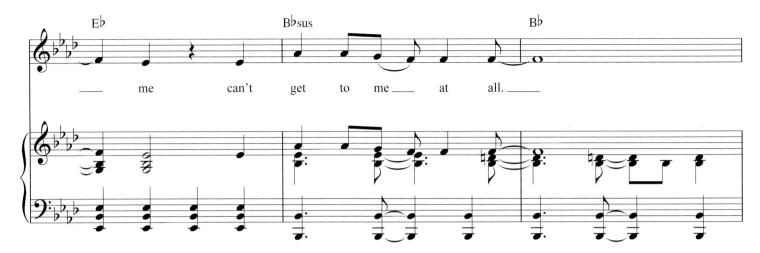

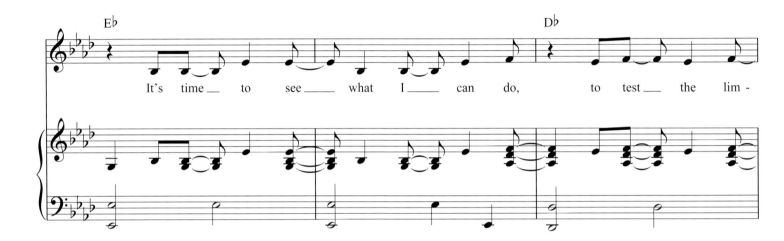

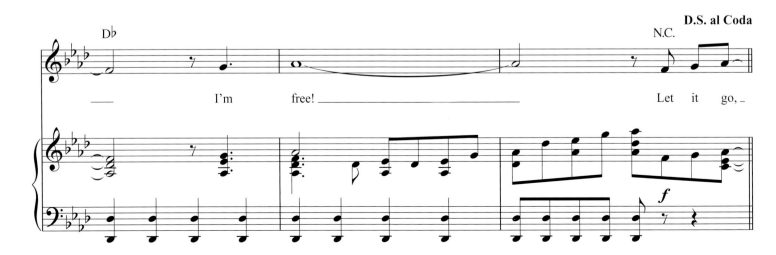

My pow - er flur -

- ries through __ the air ___ in - to __ the ground. _

My soul __ is spi - ral - ing __ in fro - zen frac - tals all __

Eb5   N.C.

_ a - round. _   And one _ thought crys - tal - liz - es like _

F   Dbmaj7

_ an i - cy blast: _   I'm nev - er go - ing back; _ the

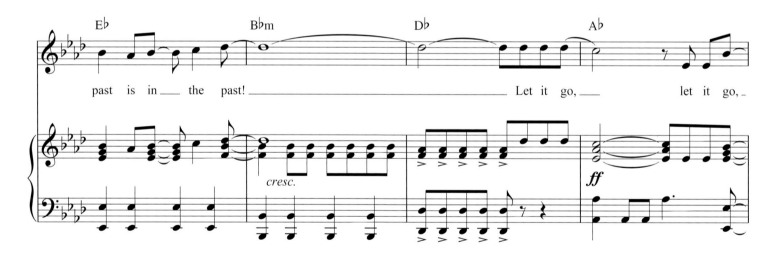

Eb   Bbm   Db   Ab

past is in _ the past! _____ Let it go, _   let it go, _

Eb   Fm   Db

_   and I'll rise _ like the break _ of dawn. _____   Let it go, _

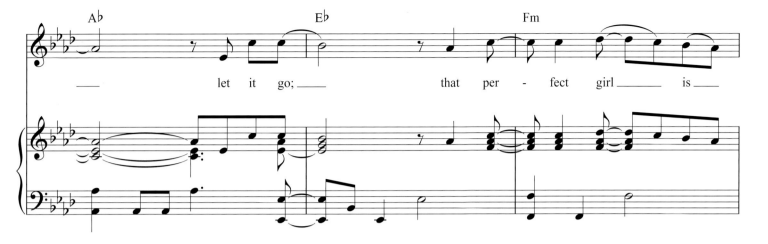

let it go; that per - fect girl is

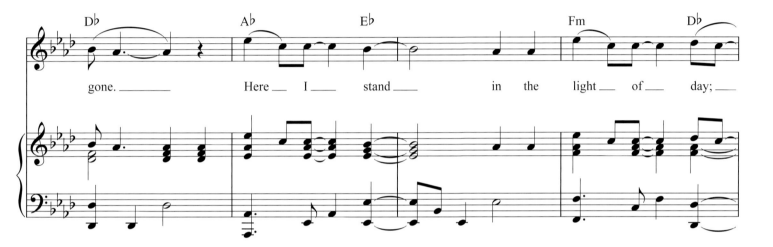

gone. Here I stand in the light of day;

let the storm rage on.

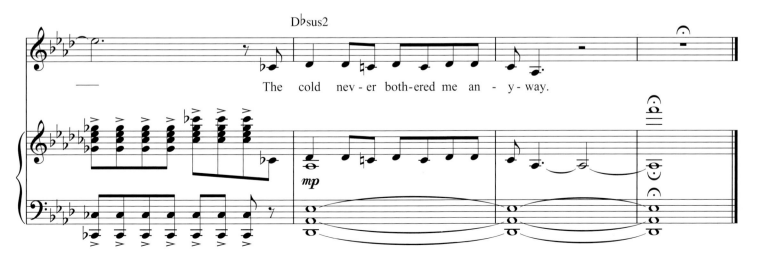

The cold nev - er both - ered me an - y - way.

Lava

From *LAVA*

Music and Lyrics by
JAMES FORD MURPHY

Easy half-time feel

Male vocal: A long, long time a-go ____ there was a vol-ca-no, ____ liv-ing all a-lone ____ in the mid-dle of ____ the sea. He sat high a-bove his bay, ____

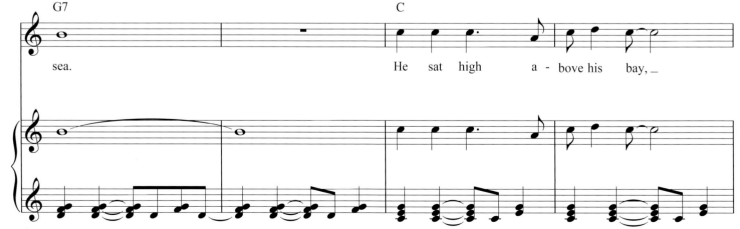

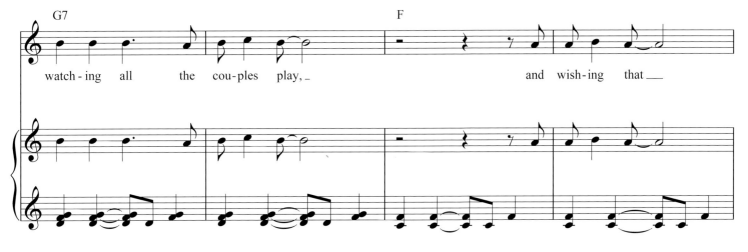

watch-ing all the cou-ples play, ___ and wish-ing that ___

he had some - one too. And from his

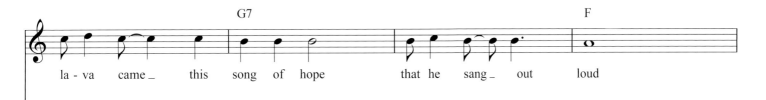

la - va came ___ this song of hope that he sang ___ out loud

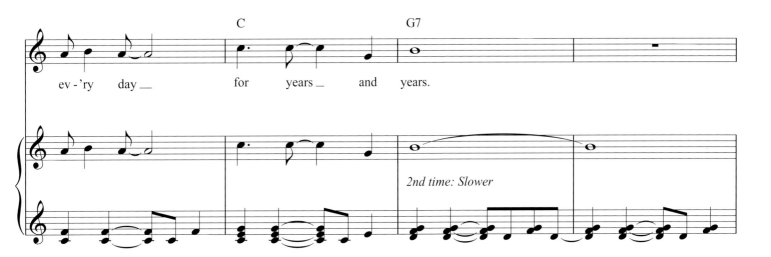

ev-'ry day ___ for years ___ and years.

2nd time: Slower

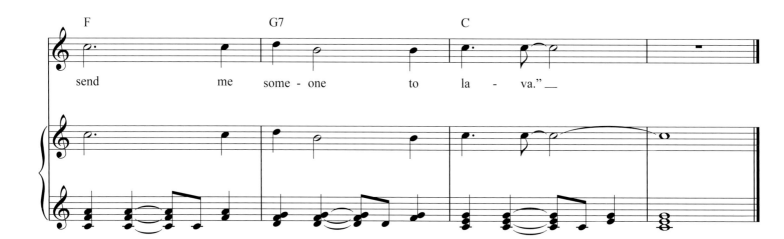

Lava

From *LAVA*

Music and lyrics by James Ford Murphy

A long, long time ago there was a volcano
Living all alone in the middle of the sea
He sat high above his bay watching all the couples play
And wishing that he had someone too
And from his lava came this song of hope
That he sang out loud ev'ry day for years and years
"I have a dream I hope will come true
That you're here with me, and I'm here with you
I wish that the earth, sea, and the sky up above-a
Will send me someone to lava"
Years of singing all alone turned his lava into stone
Until he was on the brink of extinction
But little did he know that, living in the sea below
Another volcano was listening to his song
Ev'ry day she heard his tune, her lava grew and grew
Because she believed his song was meant for her
Now she was so ready to meet him above the sea
As he sang his song of hope for the last time
"I have a dream I hope will come true
That you're here with me, and I'm here with you
I wish that the earth, sea, and the sky up above-a
Will send me someone to lava"
Rising from the sea below stood a lovely volcano
Looking all around, but she could not see him
He tried to sing to let her know that she was not there alone
But with no lava his song was all gone
He filled the sea with his tears and watched his dreams disappear
As she remembered what his song meant to her
"I have a dream I hope will come true
That you're here with me, and I'm here with you
I wish that the earth, sea, and the sky up above-a
Will send me someone to lava"
Oh, they were so happy to fin'lly meet above the sea
All together now their lava grew and grew
No longer are they all alone, with *aloha* as their new home
And when you visit them this is what they sing
"I have a dream I hope will come true
That you'll grow old with me, and I'll grow old with you
We thank the earth, sea, and the sky we thank too
I lava you. I lava you. I lava you"

How Far I'll Go

From *MOANA*

Music and Lyrics by
LIN-MANUEL MIRANDA

Moderately

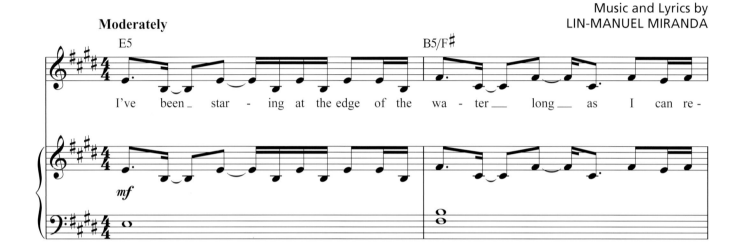

I've been star-ing at the edge of the wa-ter__ long__ as I can re-mem-ber,__ nev-er real-ly know-ing why.

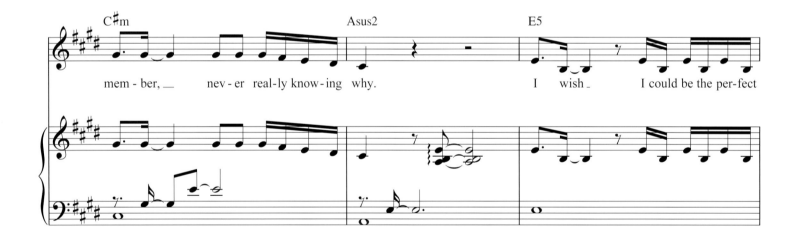

I wish__ I could be the per-fect

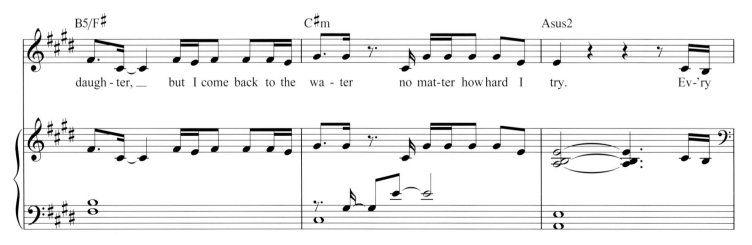

daugh-ter,__ but I come back to the wa-ter no mat-ter how hard I try. Ev-'ry

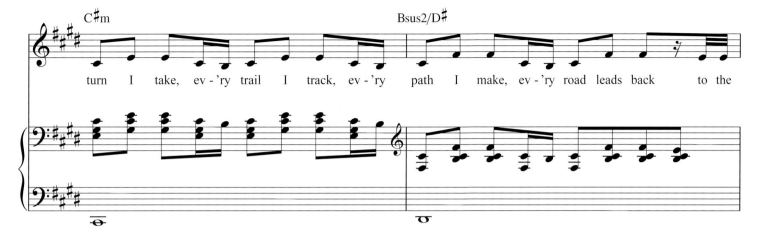

turn I take, ev-'ry trail I track, ev-'ry path I make, ev-'ry road leads back to the

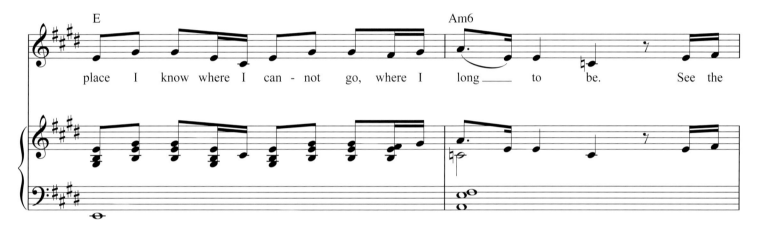

place I know where I can-not go, where I long ___ to be. See the

line where the sky meets the sea, it calls ___ me, and no one knows ___ how far it

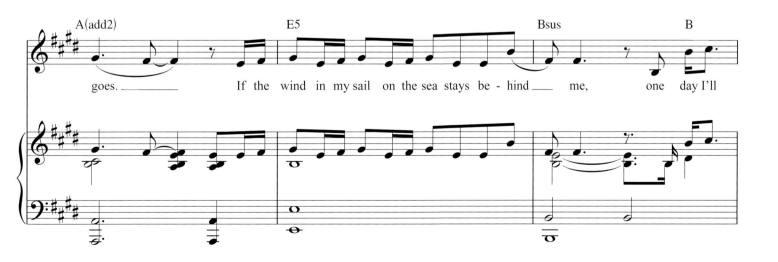

goes. ___ If the wind in my sail on the sea stays be-hind ___ me, one day I'll

know. _____ If I go, there's just no tell-ing how far I'll go. I ___ know ___ ev-'ry-bod-y on this

is - land ___ seems ___ so hap-py on this is - land. _ Ev-'ry-thing is by de-sign. _

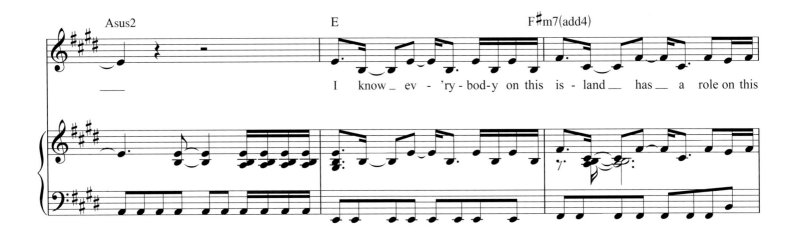

I know ___ ev-'ry-bod-y on this is - land ___ has ___ a role on this

is - land, _ so may-be I can roll with mine. ___ I can

know. _____ What's be-yond that line? Will I cross that line? The

line where the sky meets the sea, it calls ___ me, _____ and no one knows _____ how far it

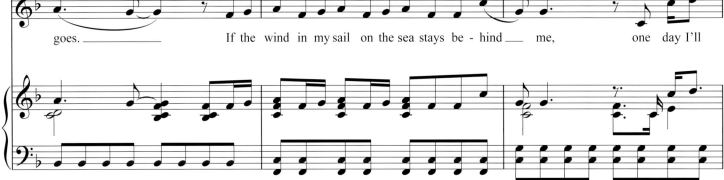

goes. _____ If the wind in my sail on the sea stays be-hind ___ me, one day I'll

know _____ how far I'll go! _____

You're Welcome

From *MOANA*

Music and Lyrics by
LIN-MANUEL MIRANDA

Moderately fast

I see what's hap-pen-ing, yeah: you're face to face with great-ness, and it's strange. You don't e-ven know how you feel. It's a-dor-a-ble. Well, it's nice to see that hu-mans nev-er change. O-pen your eyes. Let's be-gin:

Yes, it's real-ly me, it's Mau-i. Breathe it in, I know it's a lot: __

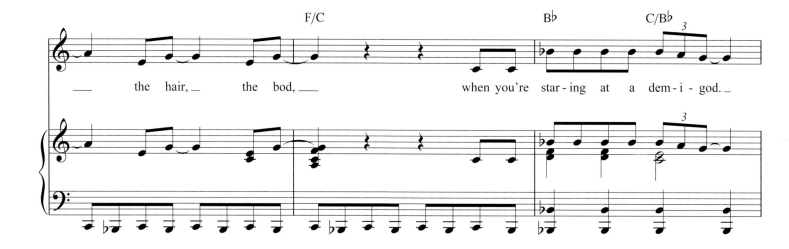

__ the hair, __ the bod, ___ when you're star-ing at a dem-i-god. __

What can I say ___ ex-cept, "You're wel - come, for the tides, __

__ the sun, __ the sky"? __ Hey, it's o-kay, __ it's o-kay: __ you're wel -

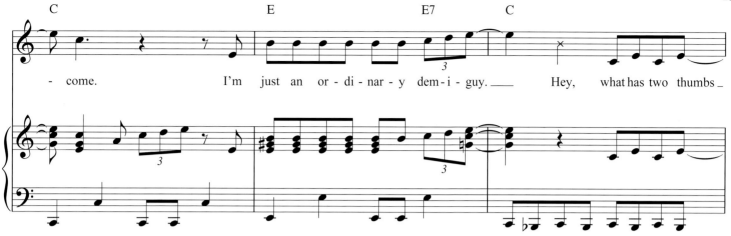

come. I'm just an or-di-nar-y dem-i-guy.___ Hey, what has two thumbs___

___ and pulled ___ up the sky ___ when you were wad-dl-ing yea high? This guy!

When the nights got cold, ___ who stole ___ you fire ___ from down be-low? You're

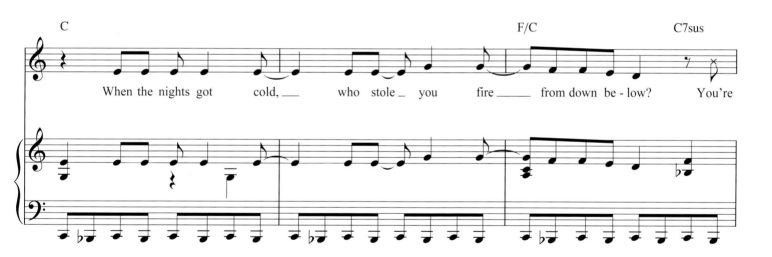

look-ing at him, yo. Oh, al-so, I las - soed ___ the sun. ___

You're wel-come. ...To stretch your days and bring you fun. ___ Al - so, I har-

- nessed ___ the breeze. ___ You're wel-come. ...To fill your sails and shake your trees. ___

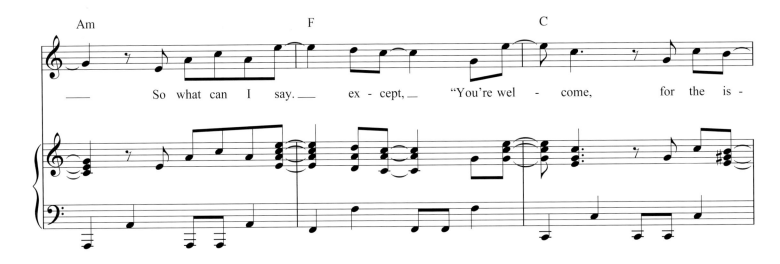

___ So what can I say. ___ ex - cept, ___ "You're wel - come, for the is-

- lands I pulled ___ from the sea?" ___ There's no need to pray, ___ it's o - kay, ___ you're wel-

-come. Huh! I guess it's just my way of be - ing me! ___ You're wel -

-come! You're wel - come! Well, come to think of it: *Rap: (See additional lyrics)*

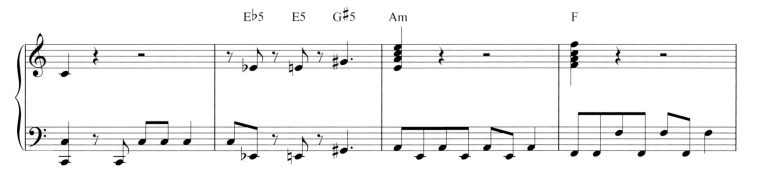

(Rap ends) Well, an - y - way, __ let me say, __ "You're wel - come, for the won -
(You're wel - come.)

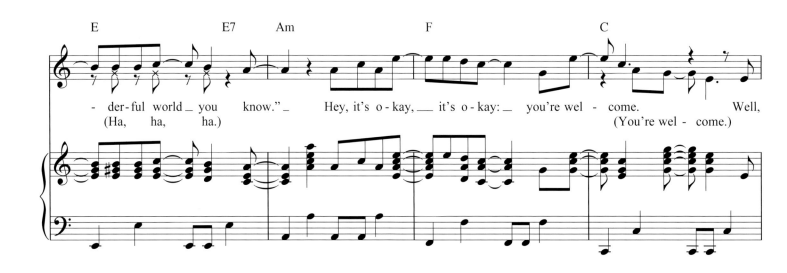

- der - ful world __ you know." __ Hey, it's o - kay, __ it's o - kay: __ you're wel - come. Well,
(Ha, ha, ha.) (You're wel - come.)

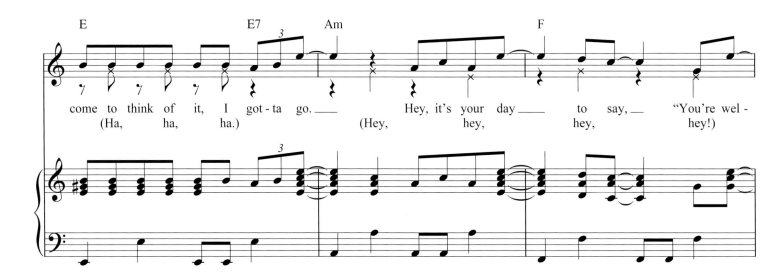

come to think of it, I got - ta go. __ Hey, it's your day __ to say, __ "You're wel -
(Ha, ha, ha.) (Hey, hey, hey, hey!)

come," 'cause I'm gon-na need that boat. I'm sail-ing a-way, a-way. You're wel-
(You're wel-come.) (Ha, ha, ha, ha.) (Hey, hey, hey, hey.)

come, 'cause Mau-i can do ev-'ry-thing but float! You're wel-
(You're wel-come.) (Ha, ha, ha, ha.) (You're wel-come.)

come! You're wel-come! And thank you.
(You're wel-come.)

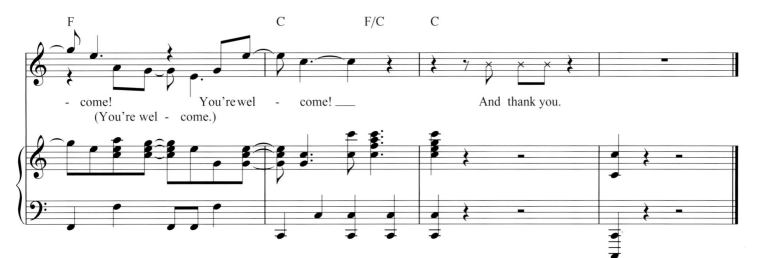

Additional Lyrics

Rap: Kid, honestly, I could go on and on.
I could explain ev'ry nat'ral phenomenon.
The tide? The grass? The ground?
Oh, that was Maui, just messing around.

I killed an eel, I buried its guts,
Sprouted a tree: now you got coconuts!
What's the lesson? What is the takeaway?
Don't mess with Maui when he's on a breakaway.

And the tapestry here in my skin
Is a map of the vict'ries I win!
Look where I've been! I make ev'rything happen!
Look at that mean mini Maui, just tickety
Tappin'! Heh, heh, heh,
Heh, heh, heh, hey!

Remember Me
(Ernesto de la Cruz)

From *COCO*

Music and Lyrics by KRISTEN ANDERSON-LOPEZ
and ROBERT LOPEZ

Moderately fast

Re - mem - ber me, though I have to say good - bye. _ Re - mem - ber

me, don't let it make you cry. For e - ven if I'm far a - way, _ I

hold you in my heart. I sing a se - cret song to you each

264

sing a se-cret song to you each night we are a-part. Re-mem - ber me, though I

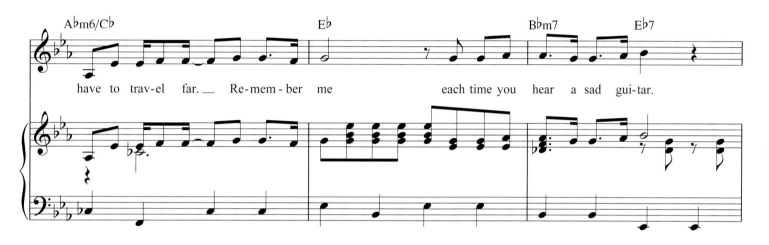

have to trav-el far.__ Re-mem - ber me each time you hear a sad gui-tar.

Slowly, deliberately

Know that I'm with you the on - ly way that I can be. Un - til you're in my arms a -

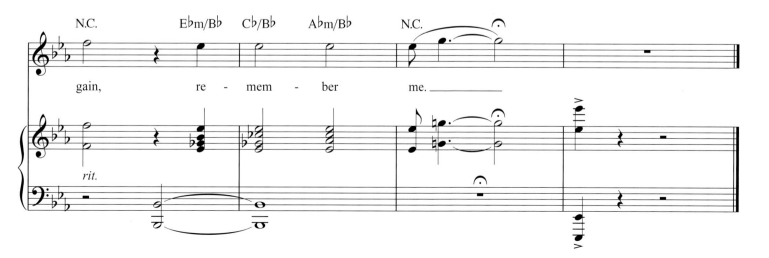

gain, re - mem - ber me.___

Let's Get Together

From *THE PARENT TRAP*

Words and Music by RICHARD M. SHERMAN
and ROBERT B. SHERMAN

Moderate Rock tempo

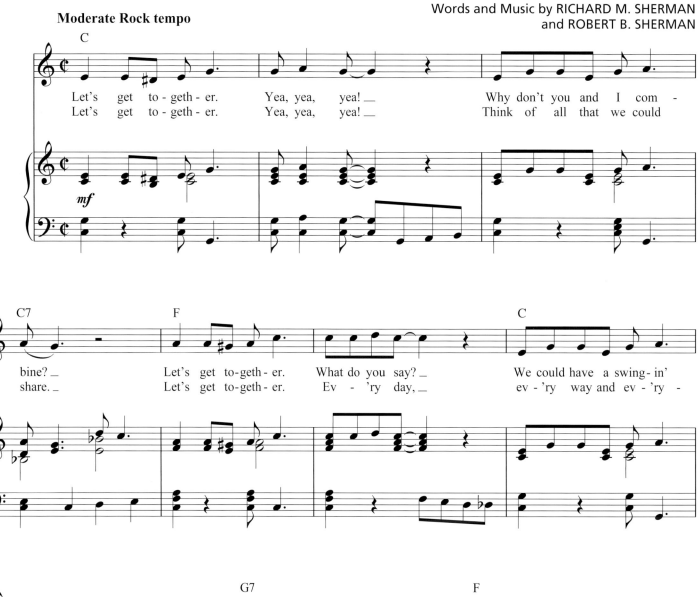

Let's get to-geth-er. Yea, yea, yea! __ Why don't you and I com-
Let's get to-geth-er. Yea, yea, yea! __ Think of all that we could

bine? __ Let's get to-geth-er. What do you say? __ We could have a swing-in'
share. __ Let's get to-geth-er. Ev-'ry day, __ ev-'ry way and ev-'ry-

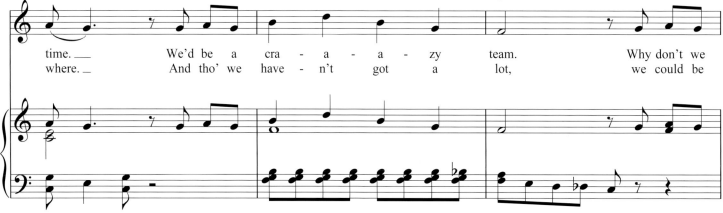

time. __ We'd be a cra- a- a- zy team. Why don't we
where. __ And tho' we have-n't got a lot, we could be

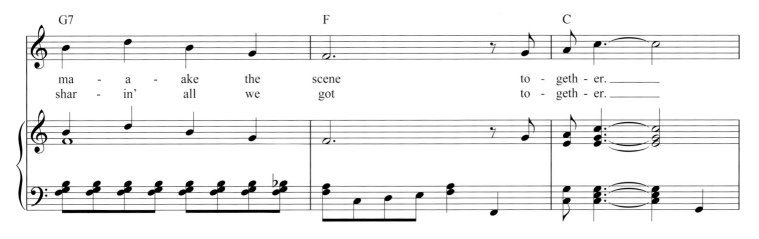

ma - a - ake the scene to - geth - er._____
shar - in' all we got to - geth - er._____

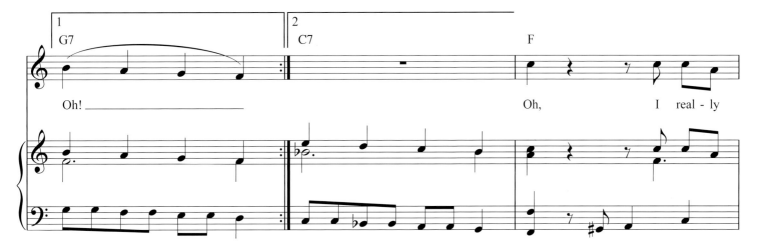

1
Oh! _____

2
Oh, I real - ly

think you're swell_ uh huh, we real - ly ring the bell. Ooh -

ee, and if you stick with me, ___ noth - in' could be great - er. Say,

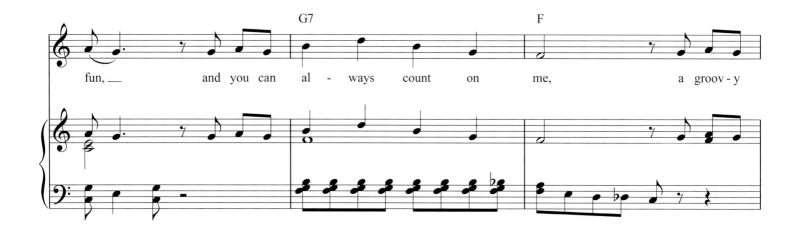

Seize the Day

From *NEWSIES*

Music by ALAN MENKEN
Lyrics by JACK FELDMAN

Hymn-like

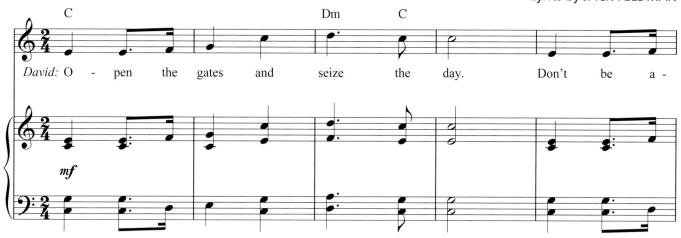

David: O - pen the gates and seize the day. Don't be a -

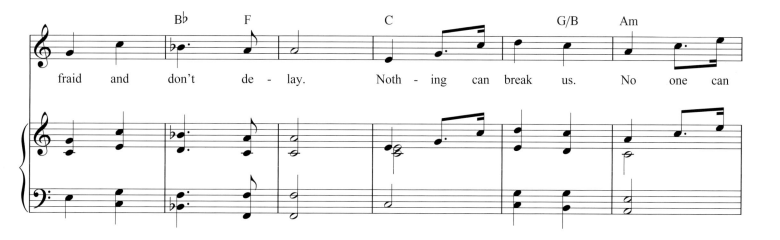

fraid and don't de - lay. Noth - ing can break us. No one can

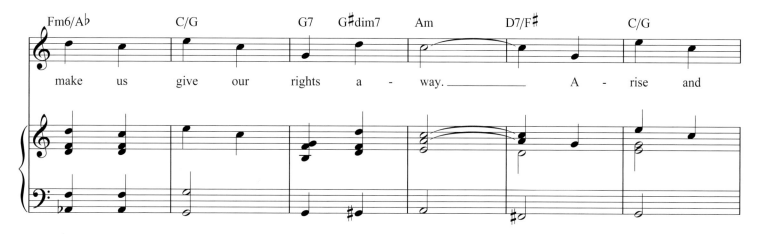

make us give our rights a - way. A - rise and

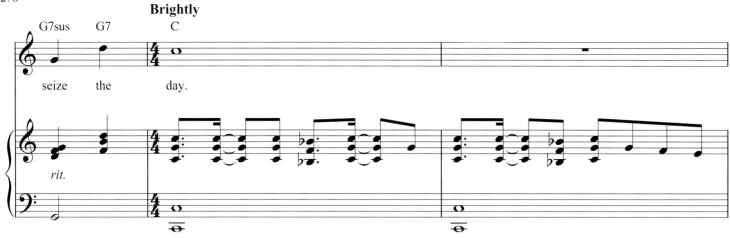

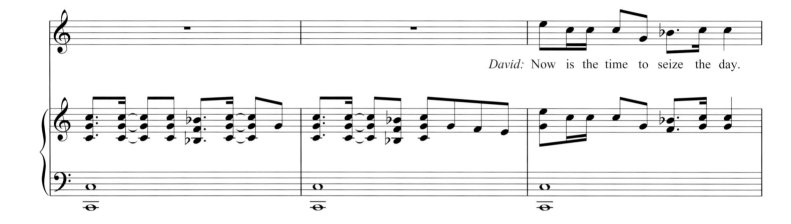

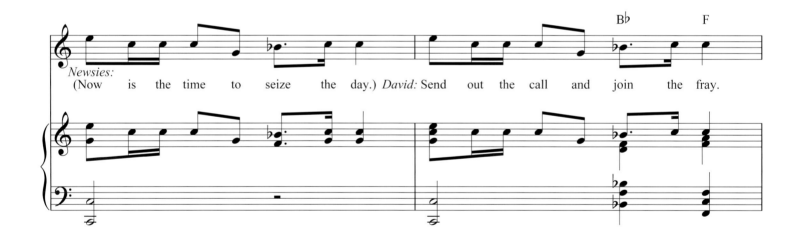

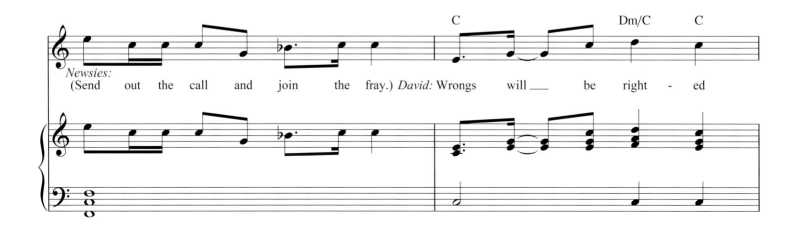

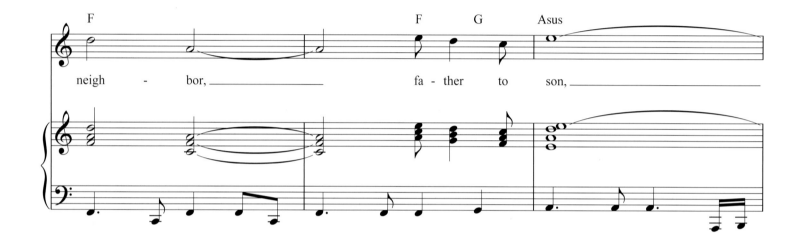

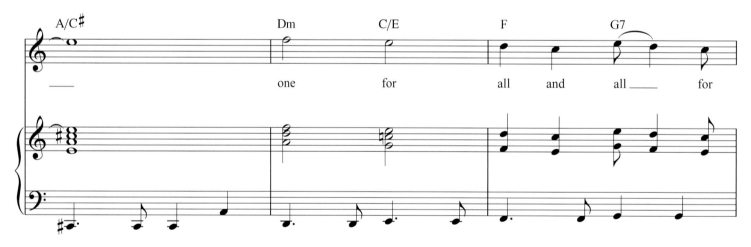

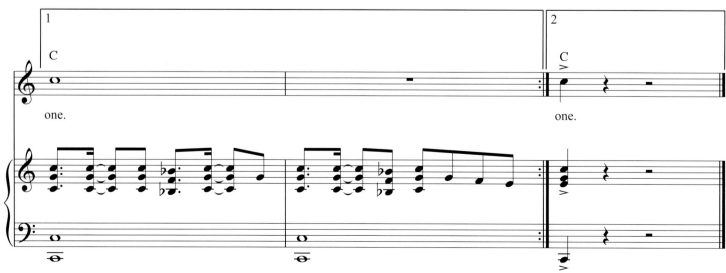

Evermore

From *BEAUTY AND THE BEAST*

Music by ALAN MENKEN
Lyrics by TIM RICE

Sturdy Ballad

I was the one — who had it all; —

I was the mas - ter — of my fate.

I nev-er need - ed — an-y-bod-y in — my life; I learned the truth — too

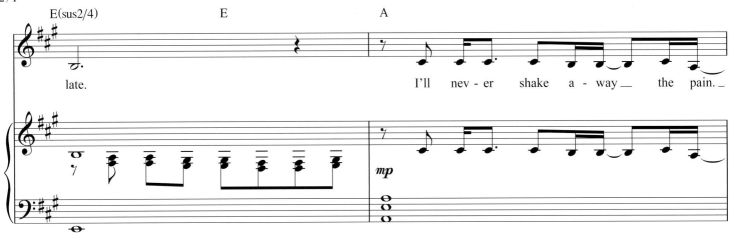

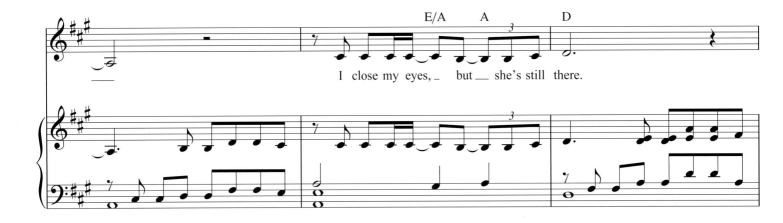

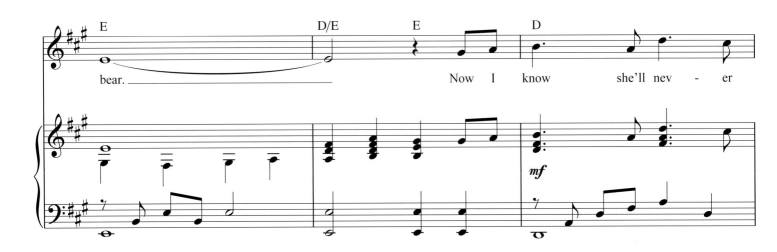

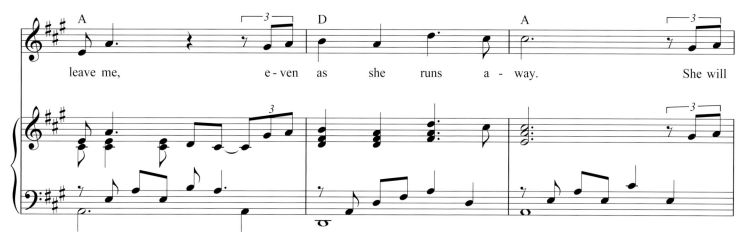

leave me, e-ven as she runs a-way. She will

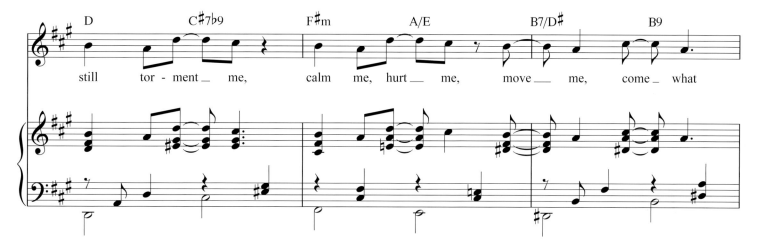

still tor-ment __ me, calm me, hurt __ me, move __ me, come _ what

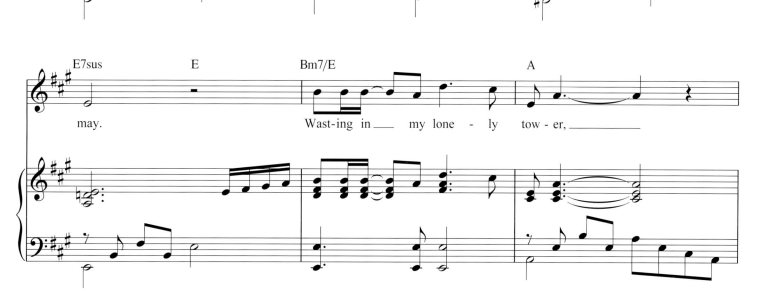

may. Wast-ing in __ my lone-ly tow-er, _____

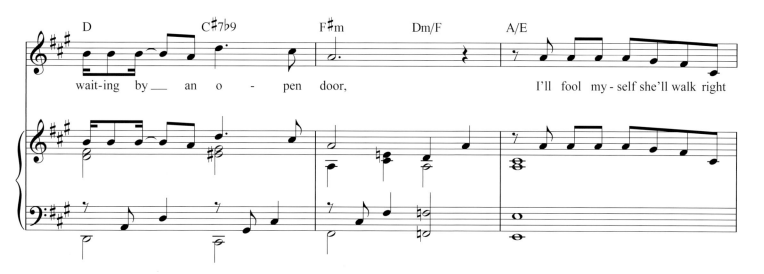

wait-ing by __ an o-pen door, I'll fool my-self she'll walk right

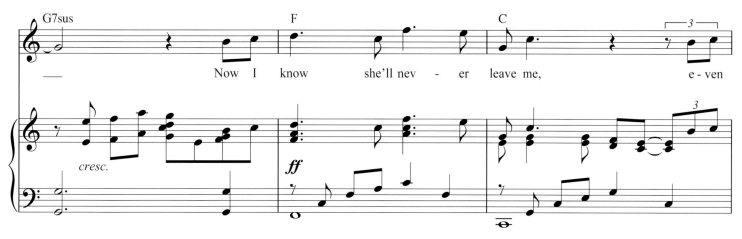

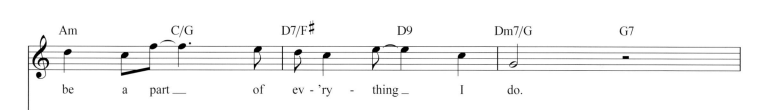

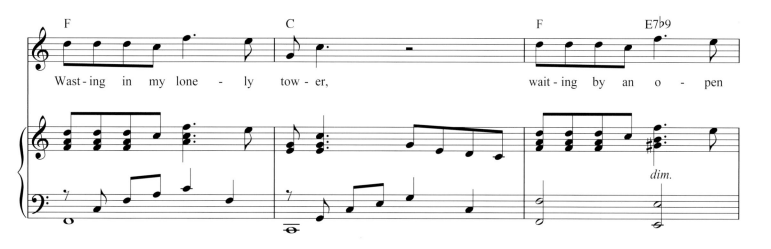

The Ballad of Davy Crockett

From *DAVY CROCKETT*

Words by TOM BLACKBURN
Music by GEORGE BRUNS

Moderately, in 2

1. Born on a moun-tain top in Ten - nes - see, green - est state in the Land of the Free. Raised in the woods so's he knew ev-'ry tree, kilt him a b'ar when he was on-ly three. Da - vy, Da - vy Crock - ett, king of the wild fron - tier! 2. In
2. eight - een - thir - teen the Creeks up-rose, add - in' red-skin ar-rows to the coun-try's_ woes. Now, In - jun fight-in' is some-thin'he knows, so he shoul - ders his ri-fle, an' off he _ goes. Da - vy, Da - vy Crock - ett, man who_ don't know fear!
3. Off through the woods he's a march-in' a - long, mak - in' up yarns an' a - sing - in' a song, itch - in' fer fight-in' and right - in' a wrong, he's rin-gy as a b'ar, an' twict as _ strong. Da - vy, Da - vy Crock - ett, buck - skin_ buc - ca - neer!
4.–10. *(See additional lyrics)*

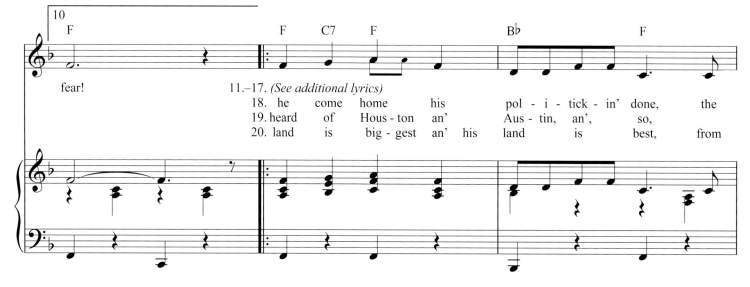

fear!

11.–17. *(See additional lyrics)*

18. he come home his pol - i - tick - in' done, the
19. heard of Hous - ton an' Aus - tin, an', so,
20. land is big - gest an' his land is best, from

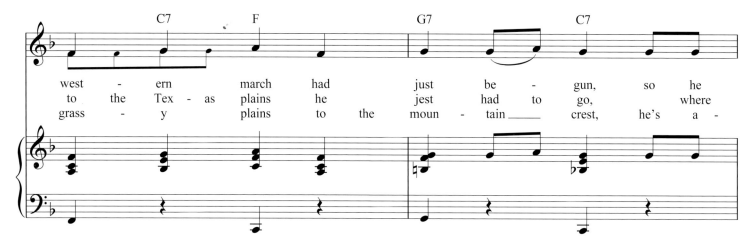

west - ern march had just be - gun, so he
to the Tex - as plains he jest had to go, where
grass - y plains to the moun - tain ____ crest, he's a -

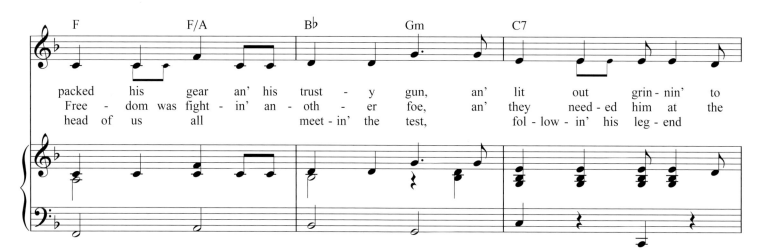

packed his gear an' his trust - y gun, an' lit out grin - nin' to
Free - dom was fight - in' an - oth - er foe, an' they need - ed him at the
head of us all meet - in' the test, fol - low - in' his leg - end

fol - low the sun. Da - vy, Da - vy Crock - ett,
Al - a - mo. Da - vy, Da - vy Crock - ett, the
in - to the West. Da - vy, Da - vy Crock - ett,

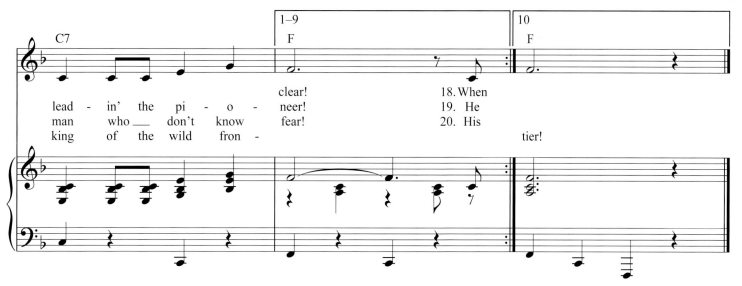

lead - in' the pi - o - neer!   18. When
man who don't know fear!   19. He
king of the wild fron -   tier!   20. His

Additional Lyrics

4. Andy Jackson is our gen'ral's name
 His reg'lar soldiers we'll put to shame
 Them redskin varmints us Volunteers'll tame
 'Cause we got the guns with the sure-fire aim
 Davy – Davy Crockett
 The champion of us all!

5. Headed back to war from the ol' home place
 But Red Stick was leadin' a merry chase
 Fightin' an' burnin' at a devil's pace
 South to the swamps on the Florida Trace
 Davy – Davy Crockett
 Trackin' the redskins down!

6. Fought single-handed through the Injun War
 Till the Creeks was whipped an' peace was in store
 An' while he was handlin' this risky chore
 Made hisself a legend forevermore
 Davy – Davy Crockett
 King of the wild frontier!

7. He give his word an' he give his hand
 That his Injun friends could keep their land
 An' the rest of his life he took the stand
 That justice was due every redskin band
 Davy – Davy Crockett
 Holdin' his promise dear!

8. Home fer the winter with his family
 Happy as squirrels in the ol' gum tree
 Bein' the father he wanted to be
 Close to his boys as the pod an' the pea
 Davy – Davy Crockett
 Holdin' his young 'uns dear!

9. But the ice went out an' the warm winds came
 An' the meltin' snow showed tracks of game
 An' the flowers of Spring filled the woods with flame
 An' all of a sudden life got too tame
 Davy – Davy Crockett
 Headin' on West again!

10. Off through the woods we're ridin' along
 Makin' up yarns an' singin' a song
 He's ringy as a b'ar and twict as strong
 An' knows he's right 'cause he ain't often wrong
 Davy – Davy Crockett
 The man who don't know fear!

11. Lookin' fer a place where the air smells clean
 Where the tree is tall an' the grass is green
 Where the fish is fat in an untouched stream
 An' the teemin' woods is a hunter's dream
 Davy – Davy Crockett
 Lookin' fer Paradise!

12. Now he'd lost his love an' his grief was gall
 In his heart he wanted to leave it all
 An' lose himself in the forests tall
 But he answered instead his country's call
 Davy – Davy Crockett
 Beginnin' his campaign!

13. Needin' his help they didn't vote blind
 They put in Davy 'cause he was their kind
 Sent up to Nashville the best they could find
 A fightin' spirit an' a thinkin' mind
 Davy – Davy Crockett
 Choice of the whole frontier!

14. The votes were counted an' he won hands down
 So they sent him off to Washin'ton town
 With his best dress suit still his buckskins brown
 A livin' legend of growin' renown
 Davy – Davy Crockett
 The Canebrake Congressman!

15. He went off to Congress an' served a spell
 Fixin' up the Gover'ment an' laws as well
 Took over Washin'ton so we heered tell
 An' patched up the crack in the Liberty Bell
 Davy – Davy Crockett
 Seein' his duty clear!

16. Him an' his jokes travelled all through the land
 An' his speeches made him friends to beat the band
 His politickin' was their favorite brand
 An' everyone wanted to shake his hand
 Davy – Davy Crockett
 Helpin' his legend grow!

17. He knew when he spoke he sounded the knell
 Of his hopes for White House an' fame as well
 But he spoke out strong so hist'ry books tell
 An' patched up the crack in the Liberty Bell
 Davy – Davy Crockett
 Seein' his duty clear!

Mickey Mouse March

From *MICKEY MOUSE CLUB*

Words and Music by
JIMMIE DODD

Brightly

Mick - ey Mouse Club! Mick - ey Mouse Club!

Who's the lead - er of the club that's made for you and me?

Hey, there! Hi, there! Ho, there! You're as wel - come as can be!

M - I - C - K - E - Y M - O - U - S - E!

E! Mick - ey

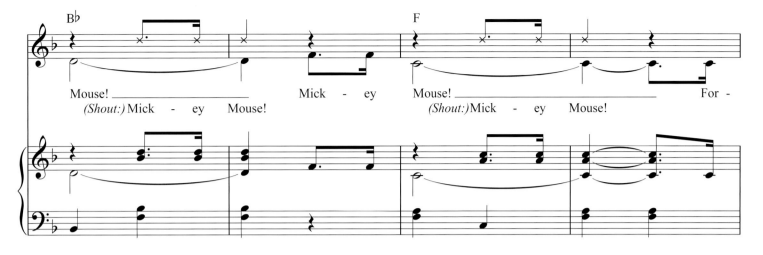

Mouse! _____ Mick - ey Mouse! _____ For -
(Shout:) Mick - ey Mouse!   *(Shout:)* Mick - ey Mouse!

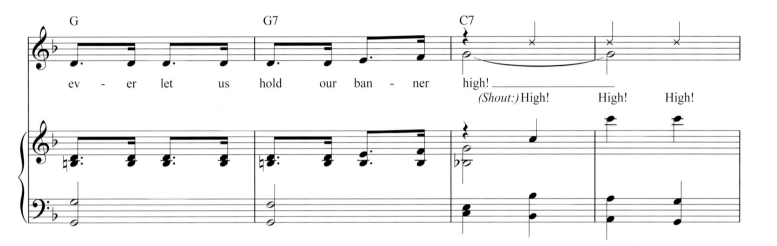

ev - er let us hold our ban - ner high! _____
(Shout:) High!   High!   High!

Come a - long and sing a song and join the jam - bo - ree!

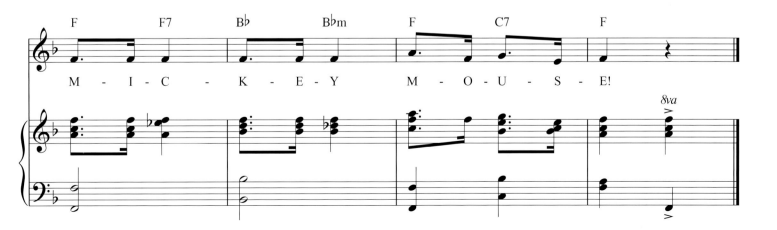

M - I - C - K - E - Y   M - O - U - S - E!

It's a Small World

From Disney Parks'
"it's a small world" Attraction

Words and Music by RICHARD M. SHERMAN
and ROBERT B. SHERMAN

March tempo

It's a world of laugh - ter, a world of
just one moon and one gold - en

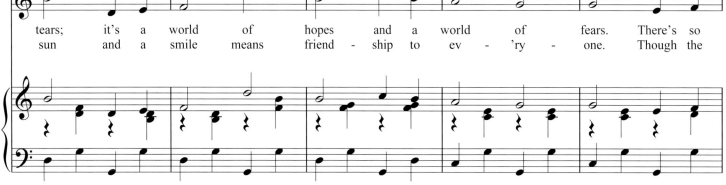

tears; it's a world of hopes and a world of fears. There's so
sun and a smile means friend - ship to ev - 'ry - one. Though the

much that we share that it's time we're a - ware it's a
moun - tains di - vide and the o - ceans are wide, it's a

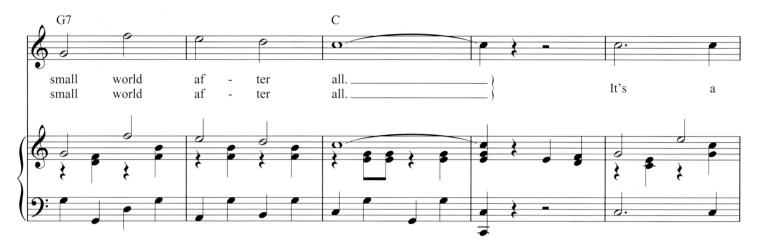

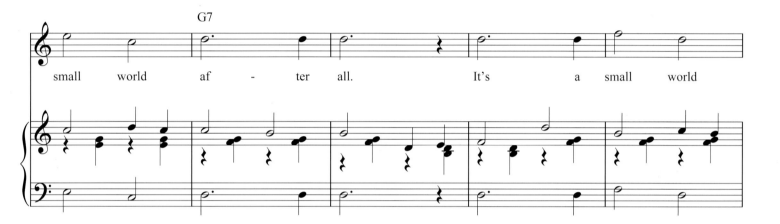

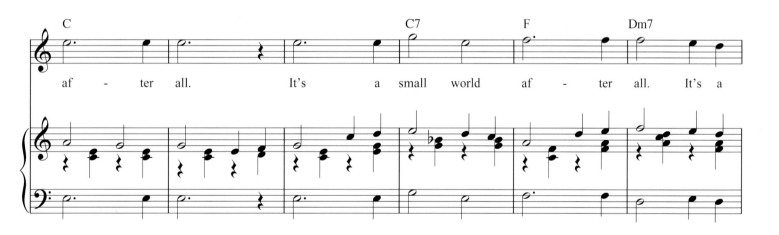

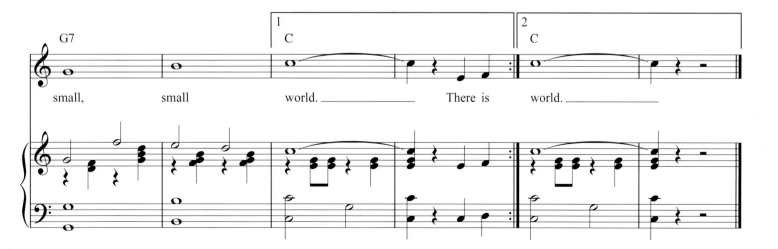

Yo Ho
(A Pirate's Life for Me)

From Disney Parks'
"Pirates of the Caribbean" Attraction

Words by XAVIER ATENCIO
Music by GEORGE BRUNS

In a robust manner

Yo ho, yo ho, a pi-rate's life for me. We
Yo ho, yo ho, a pi-rate's life for me. We
Yo ho, yo ho, a pi-rate's life for me. We

pil-lage, plun-der, we ri-fle and loot. Drink up me 'eart-ies, yo ho. We
ex-tort and pil-fer, we filch and sack. Drink up me 'eart-ies, yo ho. Ma-
kin-dle and char and in-flame and ig-nite. Drink up me 'eart-ies, yo ho. We

kid-nap and rav-age and don't give a hoot. Drink up me 'eart-ies, yo ho.
raud and em-bez-zle and e-ven high-jack. Drink up me 'eart-ies, yo ho.
burn up the cit-y, we're real-ly a fright. Drink

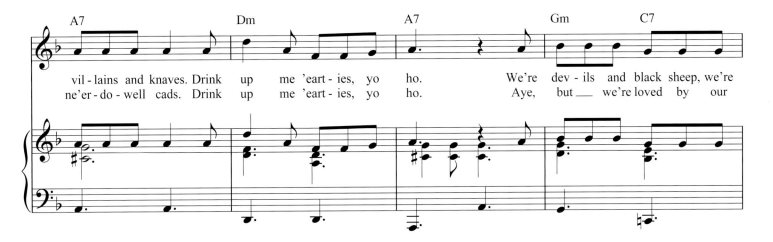

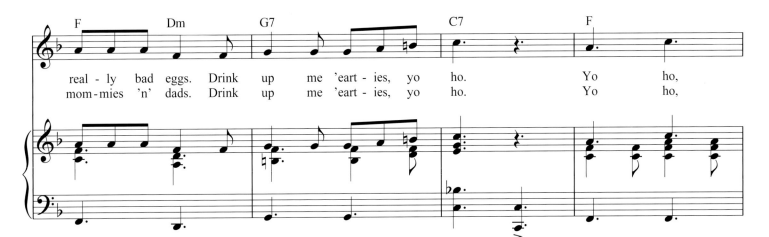

SONG INDEX